THE
RAUPŌ
BOOK OF
MĀORI
PROVERBS

A.E. BROUGHAM & A.W. REED
REVISED BY TĪMOTI KĀRETU

RAUPO

PENGUIN BOOKS

Published by the Penguin Group
Penguin Group (NZ), 67 Apollo Drive, Rosedale,
Auckland 0632, New Zealand (a division of Pearson New Zealand Ltd)
Penguin Group (USA) Inc., 375 Hudson Street,
New York, New York 10014, USA
Penguin Group (Canada), 90 Eglinton Avenue East, Suite 700, Toronto,
Ontario, M4P 2Y3, Canada (a division of Pearson Penguin Canada Inc.)
Penguin Books Ltd, 80 Strand, London, WC2R 0RL, England
Penguin Ireland, 25 St Stephen's Green,
Dublin 2, Ireland (a division of Penguin Books Ltd)
Penguin Group (Australia), 250 Camberwell Road, Camberwell,
Victoria 3124, Australia (a division of Pearson Australia Group Pty Ltd)
Penguin Books India Pvt Ltd, 11, Community Centre,
Panchsheel Park, New Delhi – 110 017, India
Penguin Books (South Africa) (Pty) Ltd, Block D, Rosebank Office Park,
181 Jan Smuts Avenue, Parktown North, Gauteng 2193, South Africa

Penguin Books Ltd, Registered Offices: 80 Strand, London, WC2R 0RL, England

First published by Reed Publishing (NZ) Ltd, 1963
Revised editions published in 1987, 1996, 1999
This fifth edition published by Penguin Group (NZ), 2012

Printed and bound in Australia by Griffin Press

ISBN 978-0-143-56791-2

A catalogue record for this book is available
from the National Library of New Zealand.

www.penguin.co.nz

Introduction

There is always reluctance, a tentativeness and a diffidence on one's part when approached to revise someone else's work. However, when one considers that this book was first published in 1963, it would seem timely that some kind of revision and extension be undertaken.

Firstly, there needed to be some consistency in the orthography and the punctuation. For instance, tribal names should be Ngāti Porou rather than Ngāti-porou on one occasion and then Ngāti-Porou on another, and surely both Māori and Pākehā, when speaking of the people, are deserving of capitals at all times?

Some way of showing vowel length had to be introduced, hence the use of the macron. There are many archaic words used in whakataukī so a way of showing how they are pronounced had to be included.

An index to the proverbs by first line and category is essential, I feel, as it avoids any frustration on the part of the person using the book.

Categorising of the proverbs also had to be reconsidered.

As the introduction to the earlier edition stated, 'The diversity of subject is considerable', and 'it is inevitable that there should be a certain amount of repetition, but the imaginative mind of the Māori provides infinite variety'. Where the repetition has been found to be unnecessary, the proverb is included once only.

Some proverbs were omitted because of their obscurity. There is little point in including a proverb quoting some ancestor's name if tribe and locality are not known or under what circumstances the quote was made.

A wealth of proverbs is available and worthy of inclusion in a collection such as this. Those newly included have been because of their interest, their beauty of language and their wisdom, much of which might seem homespun to contemporary generations, but the philosophies expounded are no less relevant, even if the language seems quaint.

To be considered a good orator, one must be able to employ whakataukī where appropriate, for they encapsulate a thought so well that there is little need to use more words when these few are so apt and succinct. For the orator's point to be appreciated, it is essential for the audience also to know whakataukī, and it is hoped that this volume might be an aid to both the orator and the audience.

MAORI PROVERBS

Principal books consulted:

Sir George Grey, *Ko nga Whakapepeha me nga Whakaahuareka a nga Tupuna*

The principal published source of Māori proverbs.

Reverend Richard Taylor, *Te Ika a Maui*

Taylor's collection was made independently of Grey and although both works have many proverbs in common, a number of further examples are included.

Transactions of the New Zealand Institute

Especially Volume 12, which includes a comprehensive selection by William Colenso. The majority of the entries duplicate Grey's collection, but new light is thrown on a number of them. Volume 22 also contains an article on proverbs and a number of examples by Judge F.H. Smith.

Reverend Reweti T. Kōhere, *He Konae Aronui*

This small book contains previously unrecorded examples, and a commentary on others. The collection is mainly East Coast in origin.

J.H. Mitchell, *Takitimu*

The book contains a further selection, again mainly from East Coast sources.

Te Ao Hou

Several issues of the magazine published by the Department of Māori Affairs contain collections by H.T.M. Wikiriwhi and Reverend Kīngi-Īhaka. Although only a small amount of new material is found here, there are some illuminating comments.

Bishop H.W. Williams, *A Dictionary of the Maori Language*

Many examples of proverbs are quoted in Māori throughout the dictionary, which has been consulted freely in order to provide fresh translations of the proverbs.

These are the principal sources, but acknowledgement is also made to the following writers among many others: Elsdon Best in *The Maori, Tuhoe* and other works; James Cowan; John Grace in *Tuwharetoa*; Leslie Kelly in *Tainui*; S. Percy Smith in *The Wars of the Northern Maori Against the Southern Tribes of New Zealand During the Nineteenth Century*; J.H. Menzies in *Maori Patterns Painted and Carved*; and to the volumes of the *Journal of the Polynesian Society*.

Tīmoti Kāretu

Ability
He ringa miti tai heke.
A hand which licks up the ebb tide.

The people of Wanganui were experienced in handling their canoes in the strong tidal waters of the river, in contrast to those who were familiar only with the more placid streams. The paddles wielded by the crews 'licked up' the outflowing tide.

Abundance
E rua tau ruru,
E rua tau wehe,
E rua tau mutu,
E rua tau kai.
Two years of wind and storm,
Two years when food is scarce,
Two years when crops fail,
Two years of abundant food.

After long waiting, prosperity comes at last.

Hare Hongi translated the saying:
Two years of insect plague,
Two years of bad weather for crops,
Two years of penitence,
Two years of abundance.

Hinana ki uta, Hinana ki tai.
Hinana to the interior, Hinana to the sea.

Hinana was the name of the pātaka or food store of the Taupō chief Te Heuheu, and was almost a synonym for plenty. It was packed with provisions such as birds from the inland forests and fish and whitebait (*Galaxias brevipinnis*) from Taupō Moana, the inland sea.

Te Wai-iti umu tahu roa.
The ovens at Te Wai-iti keep on burning.

The district was famous for its supply of birds, and the ovens were always well supplied.

Accuracy
Ko te kai a Māui, he ringaringa kau tāhanga.
The food of Māui, an empty hand.

Māui, half-man and half-god, was an adept at playing games, including ringaringa, a game in which food is held in the hand and others guess which hand is full. As Māui was always right, the proverb is applied to those whose guesses are correct.

Admiration
He whatitiri ki te rangi, ko Te Arawa ki te whenua.
As thunder in the sky, so is the Arawa tribe on earth.

There was an occasion when an Arawa war party sang a song of defiance, and the Tūhoe people expressed their admiration in these words.

Adornment
He ao te rangi ka ūhia, he huruhuru te manu ka tau.
As the clouds cover the sky, so feathers adorn a bird.

The warrior chief Tama-te-rangi had a wife who was unable to weave. He was therefore meanly clad, and for this reason he left her. On one occasion he was urged to speak, but he remained seated and uttered these words as an indication that he did not have a cloak which was worthy of display, and could not rise.

An alternative rendering is:
He ao te rangi ka ūhia, mā te huruhuru te manu ka rere.
As clouds cover the sky, so do feathers enable a bird to fly.

Adultery
Ko te wahine mā tētehi, ko te whare mō tētehi.
The woman for one, the house for the other.

Advancing in single file
Honoa te hono a te kiore.
Add to the company of rats.

Rats were in the habit of following each other along their runs.

Advantage, following up
Hinga iho, tomo atu i te pā.
With the strength of the enemy overcome, be quick to attack the pā.

Advice, parental
Kia mau koe ki te kupu a tōu matua.
Hold fast to the words your father gives you.

Advice, unwanted
Ko koe hei kī mai, mō te pōtiki whakatoatoa a Maru-te-hia-kina?
Are you a man fit to give advice to the self-confident child of Maru-te-hia kina?

Affection
Nāku anō rā tāku whakaironga.
What I fondle and nurse belongs to me.

Whāngai i tō tāua tuahine, hei tangi i a tāua.
Let us nurture our sister, and she will mourn for us.

There is comfort in the knowledge that the girl will sorrow for us if we die. It has been said that the affection of a sister is greater than that of a wife, who may marry again if she is widowed. A sister will mourn for us if we die.

Te kuku o te manawa.
The pincers of the heart.

An expression for anything that has a strong hold on one's affections.

Age
Ka eke anō i te puke ki Ruahine.
He is climbing the mountain of Ruahine.

He is growing older.

Agility
Kia tōtōia ngā waewae o taku mokopuna hai whai taki.
Let the legs of my grandchild be massaged so that he may pursue the challenger.

Māori mothers massaged the limbs of their babies from birth to make them supple. Agility was necessary when visitors came and the challenger had to be pursued and caught before he could rejoin the ranks.

Agriculture
Tēnā ko te toa mahi kai e kore e paheke.
A warrior who works hard at growing food will not fail.

Alertness
E moe ana te mata hī tuna, e ara ana te mata hī aua.
When the eyes of those who fish for eels are sleeping, the eyes of those who catch mullet are open.

The alertness of the mullet catcher is compared to those who stand on guard and are wakeful during a siege.

Ka whakarongo pīkari ngā taringa.
The ears listening like fledglings.

The saying is applied to those who are waiting impatiently for the call to a meal.

A similar expression is:
Taringa muhu kai.
Ears groping for food.

Allies
Mōtai tangata rau.
Mōtai with many men.

Mōtai, who had many friends, symbolises a tribe with many powerful allies. Mōtai was an ancestor of the Ngāti Raukawa tribe, to whom the saying is attributed. It was also applied to other tribes, for example, *Tainui tangata rau.*

Ambition
He rei ngā niho, he parāoa ngā kauae.
A whale's tooth in a whale's jaw.

If you have the tooth of a whale, you must have a whale's jaw to hold it.

ANIMATION

One must have the right qualifications for great enterprises.

He whetū ka haere ki te kai i te marama, ki te taha ki tōna hoa riri e kore rā ia e toa.
A star sets off to devour the moon but as far as its enemy, the moon, is concerned, it (the star) will never succeed.

One should realise one's limits.

Animation
E tū i te tū a Tāne-rore, e haka i te haka a Tāne-rore. Kaua i te tū, i te haka a te keretao.
Adopt the stance of Tāne-rore, and perform as Tāne-rore does. Do not adopt the stance and style of a puppet.

Advice to the men in the haka to be alive and display masculine grace, rather than be regimented, limp and wooden like a puppet.

Anxiety
Te paki o Hewa.
The fine weather of Hewa.

A proverbial saying relating to good weather when all seems well, but the heart is troubled with anxiety.

Appearances, deceptive
He kākā tino tangata.
The ugly offspring.

Appearances may be deceptive. Though they may be ugly and unattractive, they come from a line of great chiefs. The expression has the brevity and meaning of 'ugly duckling'.

Appetising food
Te iti oneone i kapunga mai i Hawaiki.
A little bit of earth from Hawaiki in the hollow of the hand.

A proverb used of appetising food secured at great cost. Hawaiki was the homeland of the race, and there are legends that tell how food, especially the prized kūmara (which was not native to New Zealand), and soil were brought across the ocean.

Appetising smell

Tēnā te kakara o Tutunui.
There is the savoury smell of Tutunui.

Tutunui was a whale belonging to the chief Tinirau, who lent it to the tohunga Kae to convey him to his home. Kae killed the whale and his people cooked it, covering the flesh with the leaves of the koromiko shrub. Tinirau looked in vain for the return of his whale, but when he smelled the roasting flesh he knew what had happened and took revenge on Kae. When koromiko branches are thrown on the fire they give out a distinctive odour which gave rise to the saying.

Appetite

Iro te iro, homai kia kainga, ka kai hoki ia i a au.
Flyblown or not, give it here to me; I will eat the maggots now, for eventually they will eat me.

The saying was quoted to one who was over-particular about his food.

Kino atu, ki te aroaro o Taiawa.
If it is very bad, bring it to Taiawa.

Taiawa was noted for his insatiable appetite.

Kia whakarongo pīkari aku taringa.
My ears hear the nestlings.

Like nestlings eagerly awaiting the parent bird.

He aha koa. Hai te tokorima a Māui.
It does not matter. I have the five of Māui.

If an apology is made for the absence of cutlery, the Māori replies that he has his fingers — the five of Māui.

Appetite, lack of

Ko te moa kai hau.
Like the moa eating wind.

Grey puts it: 'If you can live without food, you are like the moa, which always stood on one leg with its beak open, living on air.'

Other variants are:
He moa oti koe, inā te kore koe e kai?
Are you then a moa, that you don't eat?

He puku moa.
A moa's stomach, that is, lack of appetite.

Approval
Tāu mahi e te ringa whero.
Fit work for the hand of a chief.

Attendance
Te kanohi kitea o Taihakoa.
The seen face of Taihakoa.

Taihakoa was always there when needed. It is considered more polite in Māori terms to make one's requests in person rather than writing a letter. Far better to have one's face seen!

Barren country
Ko Tīreki paku kore.
This is Tīreki, which does not possess the smallest thing of value.

Tīreki was a place so bereft of anything worthwhile that there were no stones to heat the oven, and travellers had to take their own stones with them.

Beauty
Ko Hine-ruhi koe, te wahine nāna i tū te ata hāpara.
You are like Hine-ruhi, the woman who caused the wonder of the dawn to appear.

Hine-ruhi was a woman so noted for her beauty that her fame passed on from one generation to another.

Me te mea ko Kōpū ka rere i te pae.
Like the star Venus as it rises above the horizon.

The beauty of a woman is compared to Kōpū, the star that heralds the coming of the morning.

A shorter form is:
Mehemea ko Kōpū
Like Venus, the morning star.

Ko Hine-tītama koe, matawai ana te whatu i te tirohanga.
You are like Hine-tītama; the eye glistens (or fills with tears) at the sight of you.

Hine-tītama was the dawn maid, the daughter of Tāne and the earth-formed woman at the dawn of time. A beautiful woman is compared to the first girl of the dawn.

He pai kai e kore e roa te tirohanga, he pai kanohi e roa te tirohanga.
Good food does not last long; a pretty face is a sight that endures.

It may also be rendered: 'A pretty wife is better than a rich one.'

Me he aroaro tamāhine.
Like the face of a girl.

Me he takapu araara.
Like the belly of the trevally.

Me te rangi ka paruhi.
Like a beautifully fine, calm day.

Beauty, transient
He pai rangi tahi.
The beauty of a single day.

Good looks are ephemeral. It may also mean that fine weather may be followed by bad weather, or that, after a feast, there will be a famine.

Begging
Pikipiki motumotu, ka hokia he whanaunga.
He is constantly returning whenever the fire is lit to make his claim as a relative.

Used of a troublesome relative who frequently comes to share the food, but is not prepared to help in the work of cultivating it.

Toro kau mai te ringa o Pataroa.
The vain stretching out of the hand of Pataroa.

Though he begged for a gift he got nothing.

Beginnings, small
He ika kai ake i raro, he rāpaki ake i raro.
As a fish begins to nibble from below, so the ascent of a hill begins from the bottom.

Wars often rise from the most trifling causes.

Betrothal
Kua eke he taumau nā tētahi, kauaka hai raweke.
Do not interfere with those who have been betrothed.

Taumau was a betrothal ceremony observed amongst the more aristocratic families. Such unions were frequently arranged by the elders when the children were young, long before the time for marriage.

Bird in the hand, a
Ka whanga te kai ki tua o Tokarārangi?
Why wait for food beyond Tokarārangi?

Kōhere quotes the proverb, which he puts under the heading 'Bird in the hand', and says: 'Hunaara, the Horoera chief, had been to Waiapu where he had been hospitably entertained by a chief, Rahuiokehu. On his return home he invited Rahuiokehu to visit Horoera as his guest so that he might return the compliment. For a whole week a storm raged and no sea food could be procured. When the storm abated, Rahuiokehu prepared to leave for his home. When Hunaara asked him to wait so that he might be able to catch some fish, his guest uttered the above famous saying. Tokarārangi is a reef of rocks off Tauhinu Point where the sea is more or less rough. The edible seaweed, *karengo*, grows [there] in abundance . . . When in season it is easily obtained.'

Bird song
Ka ngaro reoreo tāngata, kīkī e manu.
No human voice, only the voice of birds.

Birds
Ko Tāne horo.
It is Tāne the speedy.

The birds are the children of Tāne, and the proverb makes reference to their power of flight.

Birds, flocks of
Kāore e ārikarika te tama a Tū-mataika e rere nei.
What a tremendous number of the children of Tū-mataika are flying there.

The original parent of the kākā or parrot was Tū-mataika.

Birth, lowly
Ka mahi te moenga mōkai.
Well done, you who were begotten by a slave.

Many illegitimate children and those born of slaves were anxious to make a good impression and to improve their position.

Birth, noble
Ka mahi te momo tino tangata.
Well done, offspring of a worthy man.

Bitterness
Ka katokato i te rau pororua.
I am plucking the leaves of the sow-thistles one by one.

Colenso said the pororua was the indigenous variety of sow-thistle, which was more bitter than the introduced variety called pūwhā. The meaning is: 'I hear nothing but bitter things said about me wherever I go.'

Blushes
Kei whawhati noa mai te rau o te rātā.
Like the scattered flowers of the rātā.

Rau usually means leaf, but here appears to stand for the frail red blossoms of the rātā tree, for the saying has been interpreted: 'Do not let the blushes, red as the rātā blossom, cover your face for no cause', or

BOASTING

'Do not fly in a passion for no purpose, as the wind does when it scatters the rātā blossoms'. Colenso interprets it as: 'Don't become ashamed when your lying is detected.'

Boasting
He koura koia, kia whero wawe?
Are you a crayfish, that you turn red so quickly?

A saying quoted if an enemy boasts that he has not yet been touched in the fight. The crayfish turns red when it is cooked.

He nui tō ngaromanga, he iti te putanga.
A long time away, but little to be seen for it on your return.

Whakawaewae whā.
Get yourself four feet.

Said to a boaster.

He pikitanga hoki tō te kaki.
The hard, up-hill work of the throat.

He kai ā waha.
A bragging mouth.

E whā ō ringa, e whā ō waewae.
You have four hands and four legs.

Said sarcastically. Grey puts it: 'Oh yes, you're a fine fellow I daresay — perhaps with two pairs of legs and arms.' The proverb is applied to boasters.

Boldness
Ka mahi te ringaringa aroarohaki tauā.
The hand which quivers in the face of the enemy is to be admired.

Well done, the one who is quivering his hands and menacing the enemy. The hand that holds the mere in the war dance quivers with eagerness.

Ahakoa he iti te matakahi, ka pakaru i a au te tōtara.
Although the wedge is small, by it the tōtara tree will be shattered.

Said by a chief whose force was small, but who was bold enough to oppose the might of many celebrated warriors.

The reply to this bold claim was:
Ae. Me he makohe; tēnā, mehemea he pū peka kai roto, e kore e pakaru i a koe.
Yes, it will be a good rift; but if it contains blind knots then it will never be split by you.

Bravery
Ka mahi te mea i tohia ki te wai o Tū-tāwake.
All honour to those who have been baptised in the waters of the war god.

The majority of boys were baptised at an early age and consecrated to the service of the god of war.

Ka mahi te tawa uho ki te riri.
Well done, you whose courage is like the heart of the tawa tree or, Bravo, warrior with a heart of tawa.

Ko Tū-mata-uenga.
It is the god of war.

Said admiringly of a notable warrior.

A similar proverb was:
Ko Tū-mata-whaura.
Tū of the ruddy face!

In this form the warrior's face is supposed to have become suffused with blood because of his exertions in the fight.

Ngā uri o Whakatau-pōtiki.
The descendants of Whakatau-pōtiki.

Whakatau-pōtiki was a brave leader who attacked the Āti Hāpai single-handed and burnt their famous house Te Uru-o-Manono. Another chief of this name attempted to reach Te Arawī pa at Kāwhia, which was occupied by Te Rauparaha and his Ngāti Toa. He was killed by Takiwaru, the nephew of Te Wherowhero. It is the earlier hero of this name, however, who was no doubt referred to in the proverb.

Rangitihi ūpoko i tākaia ki te akatea.
Rangitihi whose split head was bound with a vine.

Rangitihi continued fighting even after his skull had been split by the weapon of an adversary. He had it bound up with an akatea vine and, because of his courage, he rallied his men after they had retreated, and won the victory.

The proverb is also rendered:
Ko te ūpoko i tākaia ki te akatea.
The head bound with a creeper.

E, ko te matakahi maire.
Like a wedge of maire.

Maire is a hard timber which can be used for wedges to split logs. Similarly, a brave warrior can drive a wedge into the ranks of an enemy.

He kotahi nā Tūhoe e kata te pō.
A single man of Tūhoe causes laughter in the underworld.

A few brave men of the Tūhoe tribe swell the ranks of the spirits who are sent to the underworld. The Tūhoe warriors were noted for their fierceness. The remark was first made by Rangi-te-ao-rere.

He oho, ka toa a Māhanga.
An alarm — and Māhanga is brave.

A saying used of a warrior who, when the enemy suddenly appears, is eager and ready for the fight.

E! kia whakatāne ake au i ahau.
Oh, let me be a man.

When the Mātaatua canoe was drifting away, Wairaka, the daughter of Toroa the commander, made this statement as she swam to the canoe and brought it ashore. There are several different accounts of the incident which was responsible for the naming of the river, and eventually the town, of Whakatāne.

Brothers
He nui muringa hei kī mai i tōna angaanga.
The youngest born, even though an important person, must be subordinate to his elder brother.

Brothers-in-law
He taokete kai manawa.
A brother-in-law will show affection.

A man who is prepared to accept you as a brother-in-law must be fond of you.

Cannibalism
Waiho te puku nui mō āpōpō, ko te puku iti e tunu.
Let your hearty appetite wait until tomorrow; exercise the little appetite now.

On one occasion some members of a war party proposed to kill a captive and eat him. This would have been the 'big belly'; but as they had some preserved birds with them (in this case the 'little belly'), they ate them and saved the feast of human flesh for the following day.

Capture
Haere whakaparirau i a koe.
You should have gone to get a pair of wings for yourself.

Said to one who has been captured.

Carving
Ko te uhi a Tonga.
This is the chisel of Tonga.

According to Grey, Tonga was an expert carver. The proverb could possibly be applied to tattooing, because Uetonga was a chief of the spirit world who tattooed his son-in-law Mataora, who in turn introduced the art of tattooing to mankind.

Ngā mahi a Rauru.
The workmanship of Rauru.

Rauru, the son of Toi-te-hua-tahi, was credited with having originated the art of wood carving.

Ngā mahi whakairo, ngā mahi a Rua.
The art of carving is the art of Rua.

Rua brought back the art of carving from the sea god Tangaroa.

Caution
Ka karanga a Taihā, 'Kia āpititūtia, kia whano te hingahinga o ngā tūpāpaku!'
Ka karanga a Maero, 'E kāwhakina tētahi momo ki te kāinga.'
Taihā called out, 'Charge! Let us fight at close quarters, so that the enemy corpses will fall everywhere!'
Maero shouted, 'Oh, let us feign flight, so that we may bear descendants to populate our village!'

He mate i te marama.
The moon dies. A moon-like death.

Though the moon dies, it comes to life again, but you cannot return, so do not expose yourself to danger.

Challenge
Ko taku iwi tuaroa tēnā.
That is my backbone.

My backbone is sacred; do not dare to touch it.

Tukua mai kia eke ki te paepae poto a Hou.
Let them come on to the threshold of Hou if they dare.

Character
Tō te ware tōna patu he kai.
Eating is the downfall of low-born people.

Character is shown by the way people eat their food.

Charity
Kia kī rourou iti a haere.
Please fill up the traveller's tiny food basket.

He kai tangata, he kai tītongi kakī.
Another man's food is food that mocks the throat.

Chattering
He wahine ki te kāinga, he kākā ki te ngahere.
A woman in the house, a kākā in the forest.

The kākā or parrot is a noisy bird which incessantly chatters. Here, a talkative woman is compared to the bird.

He pata ua ki runga, he ngutu wahine ki raro.
As the pattering of rain above, so are a woman's lips underneath.

Before quoting this too freely, men are warned that there is a variant: *'he ngutu tangata'* — a man's lips.

Chiefs
Ko te tumu herenga waka.
The stake to which the canoe is tied.

Indicating the influence and reliability of a notable chief.

Chiefs, death of
Ko Rehua kua mate.
Rehua is dead.

Rehua is a name applied figuratively to chiefs.

Chiefs, the protection afforded by
Me haere i raro i te kāhu korako.
It is best to travel beneath the white hawk.

Kāhu korako, the term given to a hawk of light plumage, is a figurative expression for a chief. If one travels under the wing or protection of a chief, hospitality and food supplies will be assured.

Similar sayings are:
He tira parāoa, he kai te whakahaua.
Feasts are ordered wherever a chief and his followers rest on their travels.

Haere! E whai i muri i a Rehua.
Go! Follow behind Rehua.

This is often followed by:
Kia kai ai koe i te kai, kia whiwhi i te tāonga.
That you may partake of good food and have a share of the presents.

Haere i muri i te tuarā o Te Whāpuku, kia kai ai koe i te kai whakairo o te rangi.
If you travel, keep behind Te Whāpuku and you will be able to eat the rarest delicacies. Te Whāpuku epitomises all great chiefs.

He rangatira he hoa matenga mōu, kia kore koe e whakarērea.
A chief will be a friend to you at a time of disaster; he will not forsake you.

Haere i muri o te tira parāoa.
Travel in the company of chiefs.

The application today would be to travel in the company of those people knowledgeable in things Māori.

Child, an only
Tītī hua tahi.
The single egg of a muttonbird.

Childishness
He tamariki koe?
Are you a child?

Children
He iti tangata, e tupu; he iti toki, e iti tonu iho.
A little child will grow; a little adze always remains small.

Children, naughty
He pōtiki whatiwhati toki.
A child who breaks the adze.

There is no difference between children, no matter what their race. The short phrase conjures up a picture of the mischievous child playing with his father's adze so that the edge is dulled or broken. Considering the time spent in making an adze, it would be a major catastrophe in the family.

Another proverb is:
He tamariki wāwāhi tahā.
It is children who break the calabash.

He tangi tō te tamariki, he whakamā tō te pakeke.
The children cry, the adult is ashamed.

The reference is to spoilt or insolent children.

Clothes
Kia pēnei te mārōrō o tō kākahu me te mangemange.
Let your clothes be made as strong as the mangemange, which never wears out.

Mangemange is a climbing fern.

He māhiti ki runga, he paepaeroa ki raro, koia nei te kākahu o te rangatira.
A dogskin cloak over the shoulders, a fine tāniko cloak round the waist; these are proper garments for a chief.

Literally, a dogskin cloak above, and a cloak with a tāniko border below.

Clouds
Māra kūmara a Ngātoro-i-rangi.
The kūmara plantations of Ngātoro-i-rangi.

An expression for a mackerel sky, in which the clouds have the appearance of the long mounds in a kūmara plantation. Ngātoro-i-rangi was the tohunga or priest of *Te Arawa* canoe.

Clumsiness
He waewae taimaha, he kiri mākū.
A heavy foot, a wet skin.

An expression used by experts when instructing novices in the use of a taiaha, a striking and thrusting weapon. A clumsy and heavy-footed fighter ran the risk of getting his skin wet with his own blood.

Cold
Auē, taku kiri kai matai i runga o Tāpuiropa.
Alas! My skin glowed with the heat of the fire of matai wood of Tāpuiropa.

An elliptical saying in which the speaker remembers the warmth and gladness of a happier occasion, now that he is perishing with cold.

Me kauhi rānei koe ki te huruhuru kākāpo pū mai o te tonga?
Shall I cover you with a feather cloak, heaped up here from the south?

Te anu o Takurua.
The cold of Takurua.

Takurua is probably Sirius, the star which brings cold and frost and snow. The expression is often shortened to '*Te anu o Taku*'. Takurua is also the word for winter. It is believed that if Takurua shone brightly it was a sign of a severe frost.

Common property
He waka eke noa.
A canoe on which everyone may embark.

Even if a canoe was constructed by one person working alone, it was claimed as the common property of the whānau or family. Practically everything in a Māori village belonged to the family, or the sub-tribe. The only private possessions were garments, ornaments, tools and weapons.

Commoners
Kaua te ware e tū ki te marae.
Do not let those who have no position of importance or rank stand on the marae.

Low-born people should not be heard in the assembly. The marae was the open space used for meetings in the village.

He pai aha tō te ware?
What goodness is there in a commoner?

Company
Waiho i te toipoto, kaua i te toiroa.
Let us keep close together, not wide apart.

Complaining about trifles
Tīneia te ahi, auahi tahi.
Ha, he au uta. Kā pā ko te au ki Katikati, ae!
Put out the fire, it is smoking so badly.
What! It is nothing but the smoke drifting on the shore. If you were caught in the current of Katikati, ah, that would be something!

Compliment
E noho, tēnā te au o Rangitāiki, hei kawe i a koe.
O friend, remain here; the rapids of Rangitāiki will carry you on your way.

A compliment to a visitor. The saying is also used as a rebuke to a lazy person who is not taking part in paddling a canoe. An alternative version says that the north-east wind will blow the visitor on his way.

Concealment
E kore e kitea he toki huna.
A hidden adze cannot be seen.

Conclusion, false
E hoa! Rukea atu tō kura, ka nui te kura kei uta e ngangahu mai nei.
O friend! Throw away your red feather head-dress! There are many red plumes dancing on the shore!

An incident during the arrival of the *Tainui* canoe at Whangaparāoa, when the crew saw the red pohutukawa blooms and called to Hāpopo, the guardian of the kura, to throw away the prized red feathers. Disillusionment came when it was discovered that the 'red plumes' were flowers which quickly drooped in the sun. Subsequently the discarded kura was discovered by Māhina, who refused to give it up.

The incident is also ascribed to Tauninihi who, in the *Arawa* version, said:
'E, kua nui ake te kura o tēnei kāinga i te kura o Hawaiki, ka panga hoki ahau i aku kura ki te wai.'
See there, red ornaments for the head are much more plentiful in this country than in Hawaiki, so I'll throw my red head-ornaments into the water.

CONFESSION

Confession
Mehemea he raruraru kei a koe, me wewete e koe.
If you are afflicted by troubles, set yourself free of them.

During certain religious rites the person taking part would be addressed by the tohunga with these words. He then confessed any evil he had done, was freed of the consequences of his evil deeds, purified, then he was ready to proceed with the ceremony.

Confidence of youth
E tū te huru mā, haramai e noho, e tū te huru pango, hanātu haere.
Let the white hair remain here; let the black hair get up and go.

Youth takes the aggressive part in the fight.

Conformity
I ngā rā o te pai, he pai. I ngā rā o te kino, he kino.
In the day of prosperity, be agreeable. In the day of evil, be evil.

Grey translates it: 'In peace be faithful; in war be valiant'; and Colenso: 'In the good days be good; in the evil days be evil'.

Consequences
He iti te whāinga, he nui te paremata.
A little dispute, a great revenge.

Though the provocation is small, the revenge will be great.

Contempt
E kore e horo te hauhunga.
There are not enough to dispel the frost.

A remark made about a very small band of allies who had arrived to take part in a battle.

He kurī koe!
A dog, you!

A worthless fellow, no better than a dog.

Continuity

Mate atu he tētē kura, whakaeke mai he tētē kura.
A fern frond dies, but another frond rises to take its place.

Tētē kura, or fern frond, is also a symbolic term for a chief.

Engari tēnā, te tūtanga tē unuhia.
It is better that its joints are never pulled apart.

A reference to the satisfaction to be obtained from fernroot which is available all through the year, whereas other foods can be obtained only in their proper season.

Cooking

Ngahuru ki runga, ngahuru ki raro, mā te paroparo e āki.
Ten above, ten below, let the skull grind them together.

When food is not properly cooked, it has to be well chewed. Ngahuru is the old word for ten, which has been replaced in modern Māori by tekau.

Co-operation

Mā pango, mā whero, ka oti te mahi.
By black and by red the work is done.

This can be paraphrased by saying that when chiefs and slaves unite the work is soon done. Black (pango) stands for the slave who is dirty and unkempt, and red (whero) for the chief who paints himself with red ochre. Red is also symbolic of chieftainship.

He kino tokomaha ki te kai i ngā kai, tēnā kia tū ki te mahi, ka aha hoki?
When it is time to eat there are many. When it is time to work, what then?

Nāu te rourou, nāku te rourou, ka ora te manuhiri. Nāu te rākau, nāku te rākau, ka mate te hoariri.
Your food basket and my food basket will satisfy the guest. Your weapon and my weapon will dispose of the enemy.

Ko koe ki tēnā, ko ahau ki tēnei kīwai o te kete.
You at that and I at this handle of the basket.

Mā ngā raho ka tū te ure.
With testicles an erection can be sustained.

While literally and biologically true, the reference is to the fact that no man is an island — for a chief to be chief he needs people.

Courtesy
He kōtuku kai whakaata.
A white heron peers at its food.

A chief is compared to a white heron as he waits for others to be served before beginning to eat.

Covetousness
Atā, inā te kakī ka whātaretare noa, ka mārō tonu ngā uaua o te kakī.
Carefully, as the neck stretches out as far as possible, as the sinews of the neck are extended.

The covetous person is likened to one who stretches out his neck when searching for a tasty morsel of food.

He peo koe, he pītoto koe, he pīnono koe, he pirinoa koe, he kōtare koe.
You hasten, you beg, you importune, you are a parasite, you are a kingfisher.

Cowardice
He aha mā te rōrā?
What use is a coward to anyone?

He hīore hume.
A dog with its tail between its legs.

Whiore hume or *Hīore hume* is an expression meaning coward. '*He whīore hume tēnei tangata*' means 'This man is a dog with his tail tucked between his legs.'

Te waka pukatea, te waka kohekohe.
The pukatea canoe, the kohekohe canoe.

Both timbers are soft, and are like cowards who will not endure in the fight.

He tawa para, he whati kau tāna.
The pulp of the tawa berry is easily crushed.

The weak spirit of a coward is compared to the soft flesh of the tawa berry. In contrast to this the kernel is hard, giving rise to the contrasting proverb:
Ka mahi te tawa uho ki te riri.
Well done, tawa kernel fighting away.

Best was of the opinion that the timber of the tawa was indicated, and to '*He tawa para, he whati noa*', he gives the meaning, 'The brash, decayed timber of the tawa breaks easily', while of '*Ka mahi te tawa uho*', which is said of an energetic fighter, he says, 'Now is seen the strength of the heartwood of the tawa.'

Creepers
Ngā uaua o Papa-tū-ā-nuku.
The sinews of the earth mother.

Criticism
Kia eke au ki runga ki te puna o Tinirau.
I might as well be sitting on the blowhole of a whale.

The speaker is being subjected to criticism from his friends. Tinirau was the guardian of whales.

Crowds
Ka maunu te puru o Taumārere.
The plug of Taumārere has come out.

Because of this, a crowd or flood of people has come out. It is a Ngā Puhi saying which is also used in a negative form:
Kāore anō i maunu te puru o Taumārere.
The plug of Taumārere has not come out.

Ka tere Rauwa, ka tere Pīpī whākao.
Rauwa and Pīpī whakao are afloat.

Smith states that these islands on the East Coast are densely forested, and that the proverb is used of a fleet of war canoes or any large gathering where many people have assembled.
   Grey gives the proverb in an extended form:

Ka tere Rauwa ka tere Pīpīwhākao, anō ko Tūrua me he motuhanga whenua.

The islands Rauwa, on the Wairoa, and Pīpīwhākao, at Tūranga, are afloat; these islands are covered with forest trees which, seen from the mainland, look like a crowd of people, in the same manner as Tūrua looks like an island covered with forest.

Īhaka states that Pīpīwhākao derived its name through the ancestor Pawa. Whilst in search of his pet dog Marewaiteao, he passed through a block of land which is known to this day as the Aroha Block. He entered the forest and saw a whakao or a multitude of people. He had to be careful whilst searching for his dog, lest members of the tribe who were in the forest collecting tauwhara (the fruit of the kiekie), should know what he was doing. Hence the origin of the name Pīpīwhākao.

Cunning

Me te kiore haumiri kākaka.
Like a rat hugging the fence.

The kākaka was a latticelike fence designed to protect the kūmara plantations.

Me te kiore kai whata.
Like a rat gnawing the food store.

Whata, or food stores, are built on posts to protect them from rats. The simile is of a cunning rat that has managed to broach the storage platform.

Ko te tui whakapahuhu a Kahukura.
There is the slip-knot of Kahukura's string.

Kahukura was a chief who surprised the fairies netting fish one night. Up to this time men had not discovered the art of net-making. Kahukura mingled with them as they gathered up the fish and threaded the fish on flax strings, but he tied a slipknot at the end of his string so that the fish fell off as soon as they were lifted up. This so delayed the fairies that they were caught by the sun and vanished, leaving Kahukura with the net they had used.

Curiosity
He kaha ui te kaha.
One runner of a plant questions another runner.

The simile is of a person of noble descent asking questions of someone else to discover whether they are related.

Cursing
Kia mahara ki te hē o Rona.
Remember the fault of Rona.

Rona was a woman who went to get water because her children were crying at night. The moon disappeared behind a cloud, and when Rona stumbled in the darkness, she cursed the moon, which came down and took her up into the sky. She is still to be seen on the face of the moon.

Dance
Me te paihau tūruki.
Like the wing of a young duck.

The rapid movements of the hands in a dance.

Dangerous occupations
He toa piki rākau he kai nā te pakiaka.
A brave man who climbs trees is food for their roots.

A fowler's life was a dangerous one, for he always ran the risk of falling from a height and being killed.

Dark, fear of
Hokioi rere pō, pekapeka rere ahiahi.
The hokioi flies at night, the bat flies in the evening.

The hokioi was a legendary bird which could never be seen, but whose screech was heard at night. The superstitious Māori was frightened of the fearful night bird.

Day and night
Ko Tū ki te awatea, ko Tahu ki te pō.
Tū in the daytime, Tahu at night.

Tū-mata-uenga was the god of war, symbolising the manly arts practised during the hours of daylight; Tahu personified food and plenty, the leisured hours of ease, and the entertainments indulged in during the evenings.

Dead, respect for
Ka mate tino tangata, tēnā ka rewa mai.
When an important man dies, they begin to come together.

An elliptical saying which means that as soon as a notable chief dies, mourning parties begin to make their way to his village to join in the tangi, and to pay their respects to the departed, to mourn for him.

Death
He ai atu tā te tangata, he huna mai tā Hine-nui-te-pō.
Man begets, but the goddess of death destroys.

Hine-nui-te-pō, the great woman of night, is not only the goddess of death but the guardian of souls in the spirit world.

From the famous contest between Māui and Hine-nui-te-pō has arisen the saying:
Mehemea i puta a Māui i tua, kua kore te tangata e mate, kua ora tonu te Māori me te Pākehā.
If only Māui had passed through (the body of the goddess of death), then man would never have died, and Māori and Pākehā would both have lived for ever.

Me tangi, ka pā ko te mate i te marama.
Let us weep, for his is not the death of the moon.

A proverbial saying which emphasises the finality of death. According to legend, the moon revives each month in the Waiora-a-Tāne.

There is another form of the proverb, ascribed to Māui before his contest with the goddess of death:
Me matemate ā marama te tangata i te ao nei.
Let the men of this world die as the moon dies; that is, that they might come to life again.

As Hine-nui-te-pō was victorious, man's death became final.

Te tatau o te pō.
The door of the night.

A figurative expression. Pō is the spirit world.

Kai raro te rua o te mate, arā, kai a Papa; kai runga te rua o te ora.
The realm of death is below with Papa the earth mother, the realm of life is above.

Papa represents the female element, which symbolises death, while life was represented by the gods, of whom Rangi was the sky father. *See* Life and Death.

Ehara i te tī e wana ake.
It is not like the ever-renewed shoots of the cabbage tree.

Death is final and irrevocable. The tī or cabbage tree is hard to kill, because new shoots spring from apparently dead trunks.

Death, different kinds of

He toa taua, mate taua; he toa piki pari, mate pari; he toa ngaki kai, mā te huhu tēnā.
A warrior dies in battle; a man who climbs cliffs dies on a cliff; a man who cultivates food dies of natural causes.

It is left to the imagination which is the best death, but the Māori had no doubt. The death of a warrior was to be greatly desired.

Mate i te tamaiti he aurukowhao, mate i te whāea he tākerehāia.
Death of a child is like a leak in a canoe, but the death of a mother is like an open rent in the bottom of the canoe.

Death of a chief

Ko Rehua kua mate.
Rehua has been overcome by death.

Once again we see the figurative use of the name Rehua for a chief.

Ka hinga te tōtara o te wao nui a Tāne.
The falling of the tōtara tree in the great forest of Tāne.

DECEIT

Kātahi anō ngā tai o Maihirangi ka ngunguru.
At last the tides of Maihirangi are moaning.

A Ngā Puhi saying used at the death of a chief.

Deceit
Ko Māui tinihanga koe.
Like Māui, you are a deceiver.

The proverb may have arisen from the action of Māui who went to his grandmother Mahuika, the goddess of fire. She gave him fire from her fingernails, but each time Māui deceived her by pretending that the fire had gone out, and asked for more. His grandmother's patience became exhausted. She set the forest on fire and Māui was lucky to escape. 'Seeds of fire' remained in the kaikōmako and other trees which were used by the Māori for kindling fire.

He kōrero kei runga, he rahurahu kei raro.
While the top is speaking, the bottom is meddling.

While the mouth is speaking smooth words, the hands are being used to rob.

Ko Warahoe te awa, ko warahoe te tangata.
Warahoe is the river, deceitful are the people.

A punning proverb about the sub-tribe which took its name Warahoe from the stream, later called the Ōrini. Warahoe means deceitful.

He pounamu kākano rua.
A double-grained piece of greenstone.

Īhaka says that the modern interpretation of the saying is a 'two-faced' person. It is also applied to those who are subject to varying moods.

Defeat
He toa paheke te toa taua.
Slippery or uncertain is the fame of the warrior.

No matter how great his power, in the end he will be vanquished, for he stands on an insecure footing.

An extended version says:
Tēnā ko te toa mahi kai e kore e paheke .
But the industrious cultivator will never slip.

Hoki atu i konā, ka tū ngā tai o Rākei mata taniwha rau.
You had better go back, for where the waves break on Rākei, the eyes of many taniwha are waiting.

Rākei is a cliff against which the waves beat. The proverb originated in the escape of a woman from her husband. She managed to skirt the cliffs before the tide came in. When her husband arrived, it was too late for him to pass, and she taunted him with these words.

Another version, referring to the same incident, reads:
Hoki atu i kona, ko te manu i motu i te māhanga e kore e taea te whai.
Go back from where you are, for it is useless to pursue the bird escaped from the snare.

Honoa te pito ora ki te pito mate.
Join the living end to the weak one.

Ultimate defeat may be avoided if a man contrives to marry the daughter of the man who overcame him. Their offspring will never be insulted by references to their father's defeat. The analogy probably comes from the planting of kūmara. If one tuber appears unhealthy, another is planted in the mound to make sure of the result.

Hā, hā, pakapaka ana Maru-whaka-aweawe.
Ha! Maru-whaka-aweawe is completely done for.

The saying commemorates a dramatic moment when the chief Maru-whaka-aweawe, engaged in hand-to-hand combat, was surprised by being thrust through the body with a spear. He turned his head, saw the spear-point protruding through his back, and uttered these words.

Defence
He umauma tangata, he umauma rākau.
A human breast, a wooden breast.

The courage and steadfastness of men and the stalwart palisades of the pā together are invincible.

DEFIANCE

Kia huhua ngā pā o Toi-te-hua-tahi.
Let there be many fortified villages of Toi-te-hua-tahi.

Toi-te-hua-tahi was the Polynesian voyager who landed in the Bay of Plenty in the twelfth century.

Defiance
Kei mate ā tarakihi koe, engari kia mate ā ururoa.
Do not die like the tarakihi, but rather like the shark.

Put up a struggle to the very end. The tarakihi is a fish which does not put up a fight when caught, whereas the shark is a fighter to the very end.

There is a more succinct form of the proverb:
Kia mate ururoa te tangata.
A man should die game like the shark.

Haere mai, ki te ururua i Wharekura, ki te puna whakatotō riri.
Come to Wharekura, where warriors stand like rank growth, to the spring which gushes battle.

I taka ko ia i te pari me tere moe ko ia.
One might fall off a cliff if one went walking about in one's sleep.

A sleep-walker might fall off a cliff and could be robbed with impunity; but he who is wide awake will defend his possessions.

Te whakangungu nei ki nga tara-ā-whai o Ārai-te-uru.
The warding off of the sting of the stingray at Ārai-te-uru.

In this case Ārai-te-uru is not the celebrated early canoe, but a shoal near the mouth of the Waitara River in Taranaki. Stingrays are frequently found in tidal waters. The proverb is applied to a man who by his boldness defends his tribe against others.

Waiho ia i konā toa mai ai. Ka taka mai ia ki ngā kākā ngau popo a Haeana, ka mate ia.
Let them be brave. If they encounter the parrots of Haeana, which rend rotten wood, they will die.

Haeana had been warned that a war party was approaching, and that it was noted for its ferocity. This was his reply.

Depression
Tiwhatiwha te pō, tiwhatiwha te ao.
Gloom and sorrows prevail, day and night.

Derision
Ko Tāwhaki koe.
You are Tāwhaki.

Tāwhaki was the notable demi-god who had many fabulous adventures on earth and in the sky.

Another rendering is:
Ko Whakatau-ihu koe.

Ka riri Taihā, ka kata a Maero.
Taihā is angry, but Maero only laughs.

Hare Hongi expanded this to: 'He puts forth his great strength in vain, and is angry, whereupon the weak ones laugh'.

Descent, pride of
Te ūpoko whakahirahira o Rangitihi.
The illustrious head of Rangitihi.

Rangitihi's head was tapu or sacred, and therefore no one dared treat his descendants disrespectfully. To curse them would bring trouble.

Deserted village
Kua pīreretia te kāinga.
The settlement has been deserted.

Desertion
Kua pae nei hoki te kōputunga ngaru ki te one.
The sea foam has been cast ashore and is lying in heaps on the beach.

Said by an elderly wife whose husband has neglected her for a younger woman. The white sea foam is a simile for the white hair of age.

DESOLATION

Te uri o Tūtāria whakarere tangata.
The offspring of Tūtāra, deserter of mankind.

Used of those who desert one in time of need.

Desolation

Kia pēnā tō kāinga, tupuria ana e te mauti.
In the same way your village will become overgrown with weeds.

Your village will be taken and will become covered with the undergrowth which springs up so quickly.

Hāhā te whenua, hāhā te tangata.
In a desolate land, man is deserted.

Despair

Ka whatiwhati koa ngā parirau o Rupe.
The wings of Rupe are quite broken.

Rupe was the form of a pigeon into which Māui changed himself. The meaning is that the men of the tribe are all dead or departed.

Desperation

Waiho kia oroia he whati toki nui.
Never mind, let the adze be sharpened by breaking it.

If the edge of the adze is chipped, it can be sharpened and made keener than ever. If most of the warriors are killed, those who remain will be fiercer than ever.

Determination

Ka mārō te kakī o te kawau.
The neck of the shag is stretched out.

A kawau mārō is a compact body of warriors ready to charge. Men are ready and eager to leap into battle, as a shag is ready to take flight when its neck is stretched out.

He rāngai maomao ka taka i tua o Nukutaurua, e kore a muri e hokia.
A shoal of maomao that has once turned round the point Nukutaurua will never turn back.

Kaua e hoki i te waewae tūtuki, ā pā anō hei te ūpoko pakaru.
Never turn back because of stumbling feet, but only because of a broken head.

Dexterity
Ka tau anō tō rākau e kuku nei i te tangata.
No wonder your weapon cuts off the breath of man.

Said in admiration when the chief Te Iwi-tua-roa gave a display of his skill in brandishing a taiaha.

He ringa whiti.
The first blow.

A common saying is '*Māna te ringa whiti*' — Let him strike the first blow.

Diet, change of
Ka mahi koe, e te waha kua kerakera.
Well done, mouth that has become nauseated.

An exclamation of satisfaction when a change of food is at last achieved.

Diet, staple article of
Te tūtanga tē unuhia.
The portion that can never be withdrawn.

This was fernroot, the essential article of diet which never failed, and could be gathered at any time of the year.

Difficulties, overcoming
He manga wai koia kia kore e whitikia.
It is a big river indeed that cannot be crossed.

Make light of difficulties and they will disappear.

Disappointment
Mānawa te taonga o te pā!
Behold the treasure of the village!

Grey explains that it is an ironic expression, used when one is disappointed at the small value of a gift.

Pōhēhē noa te tamāhine a Rangi-monoa ki tēnei tauparapara.
The daughter of Rangi-monoa was misled in coming to this ridge covered with trees.

Parapara was a tree. Rangi-takahi-wai had gone up the Whakatāne Valley to make a home for herself, but she was so disappointed by the steep, densely forested sides of the Mahaki-rua stream that she made this statement and returned to the coast.

Disaster
Mōku anō ēnei rā, mō te rā ka hekeheke, he rākau ka hinga ki te mano wai.
For me these days, for me the setting sun, for the tree that will be swept away in the flood waters.

Mano wai or deep-running water is a figurative expression for disaster. The proverb is a plea for kindness and understanding in the last days of old age. Colenso relates an amusing episode when, in 1852, Donald McLean paid Te Hāpuku for Māori land at Hawke's Bay. An old chief, Te Weretā, quoted the proverb and was given a lion's share of the money — and lived for a further twenty years to enjoy it.

Discourtesy
He tangata takahi manuhiri, he marae puehu.
A man who eats with visitors without being invited to do so causes dust to rise in the courtyard.

It was customary for hosts to see that their guests were fed before they sat down to eat themselves. Takahi means to trample or plunder, but the expression takahi manuhiri is used in the sense of eating with a guest without being invited to do so.

Discretion
He taonga nui te tūpato.
Discretion is an important asset.

Discretion is the better part of valour.

He oma a Tawheta i ora ai.
By running away Tawheta saved himself.

He maire tū wao mā te toki e tua.
A maire tree in the forest can be felled with the axe.

Discussion
Tā te rangatira, tāna kai he korero, tā te ware he muhu kai.
The food of the noble chief is discussion, but the commoner will be bored.

Apparently a play on words. Muhu kai is 'stupid food' or the food of stupidity, while muhukai means inattentive.

Me he maonga āwhā.
Like a lull in a rainstorm.

Applied to a sudden pause in a debate or argument.

Disease
He taru tawhiti.
A thing from afar.

A modern saying. In his natural state the Māori was prone to few diseases, but after the coming of the European they fell victim to tuberculosis, measles, and many other complaints which were brought from overseas.

Disillusionment
Haere ana Manawa-reka, noho ana Manawa-kawa.
Sweet-heart goes away, Bitter-heart remains.

One who has obtained what he wants goes away well pleased, but one who has trusted to another's promise and has been disappointed remains with an aching heart.

Dispersal
Ka rere te uri o te tangata, ki wīwī, ki wāwā.
The human race has fled to Wīwī and Wāwā.

According to Grey, Wīwī and Wāwā were two islands somewhere in the Pacific Ocean which the ancestors of the race often visited before they came to New Zealand. However, the statement is open to doubt. Wīwī and Wāwā means here and there, or hither and thither. The meaning of the proverb is simply that a tribe or a large body of men has been dispersed or destroyed.

Leslie Kelly quotes the saying of Heta in Hawaiki:
Mā te aha koe e kawe ake ki reira, ki te kāinga o te wīwī, o te wāwā, o te tūmatakuru, o te ongaonga?
What will conduct you to there, to the abode of indefinite location, of thorny shrubs and stinging nettles?

Distance
Kai Hawaiki noa atu ahau e noho atu.
I am sitting far away at Hawaiki.

Hawaiki was the homeland of the Māori race, and was a far-off place. The expression was sometimes used figuratively; for example, Best says that he heard these words used by a Māori who was invited to seat himself closer to the fire.

Disturbance, avoiding
Tunu huruhuru, kei wawe tū ana a Pū-whakaoho.
Cook it with its hair on, lest you be interrupted by Pū-whakaoho.

The suggestion is that the rat be cooked with its hair on in case someone should disturb the eaters.

Diversity
Ko Awa whare rau.
There are many houses of Ngāti Awa.

Ko Waitaha ngā tangata, ko kawe kē te ngakau.
All men of the Waitaha tribe, but all differing in inclinations.

Doubt
Ko tō kai waewae te tuku mai ki a au, kia huaina atu e arotau ana mai.
You allow your feet to come here to visit me, that it may appear to others as if you were glad to come.

Usually said by a woman who doubts her lover's affections; sometimes by people of the village who doubt the integrity of a visitor.

Durability
He peka tītoki e kore e whati.
A branch of the tītoki tree will not break.

Like a tough branch of this wood.

E kore e ngawhere, he maire tū wao, mā te toki e tua.
A maire tree standing in the forest will not give way; only by means of the adze can it be felled.

A saying used of men as well as of timber.

Duration, short
He harore rangi tahi.
A mushroom of a single day.

A saying applied to anything short-lived, or not long established.

Eagerness
E ai ō harirau?
What wings do you have with which to fly here?

He whakatau karanga, tino taka iho a Te Kahu.
As soon as the call to food is given, Te Kahu rushes in.

Used of a person who interprets a compliment too literally, or who accepts an invitation too eagerly.

Early influences
Nā te moa i takahi te rātā.
The rātā which was trodden on by a moa (giant extinct bird) when young will never grow straight; so early influences cannot be altered.

He tangata i akona ki te whare, tūnga ki te marae tau ana.
A person taught at home shapes well on the marae.

Early rising
E mua āta haere, e muri whatiwhati waewae.
Those who rise early in the morning are first; late risers have to bend their legs quickly to catch up.

A shorter form:

E mua āta haere, e muri tata kino.

Kōhere translates as: To start early is leisurely going, to start late is breakneck.

Similarly:

E mua kaikai, e muri kai hūare.

It's the early ones who get the best food, the late ones get the spittle.

Eating

He kūkū tangai nui, he kākā kai honihoni.

A pigeon has a big crop, a parrot nibbles at its food.

Applied to a person who eats in a leisurely manner.

Te kakī wurua āu mahi.

Your work is that of the revelling throat.

Ecstasy

Tāu mahi rā, e te iti kahurangi!

Well done, you little beauty!

A colloquial but accurate rendering for kahurangi is a treasured possession, a jewel, or darling.

Eloquence

Me he korokoro tui.

Like the throat of a tui.

The tui or parson-bird is renowned for its song, to which the voice of an eloquent orator or a sweet singer is compared.

Elusiveness

Ko Tangaroa ara rau.

Tangaroa of the many paths.

Tangaroa was the god of fishes, and the saying refers to eels, which so easily escape fishermen and eel weirs.

Encouragement
Ehara i te aitanga a Tiki!
Well done, O descendant of Tiki!

This was an exclamation of encouragement.

Energy
Ngāti Maru rangi tahi.
Ngāti Maru of a single day.

Best describes the proverb as an illustration of Ngāti Maru energy and strenuous activities: 'They would perform great feats within the space of a single day, travel long distances over their rugged lands, throwing the miles behind them as does the sun, or consume an immense *tahua* (heap of food), ere the sun went down upon their wrath.'

Enjoyment
Mā roto rā e kata.
Let inside me laugh.

Kōhere quotes this Ngāti Porou expression, which is used of one who does not show his enjoyment outwardly.

Environment
E hoki te pātiki ki tōna puehutanga?
Does the flounder return to the mud it has stirred up?

E kore te pātiki e hoki anō ki tōna puehu.
A flounder will not go back again to the mud it has stirred up. This may be a metaphorical rendering of escaping from the past.

Escape
Ko Tangaroa pūkanohi nui e kimi putanga ana.
The big eye of Tangaroa keeps on looking for a place to escape.

Tangaroa was the god of fishes. Elsdon Best puts these words into the mouth of a fishing expert who swam out to the centre portion of a seine net and got the other fishermen to lift it so that some of the fish could escape, and so prevent the net from tearing. As he swam amongst the fish, which included sharks, he knew he was in no danger because they were too intent on escaping to attack him.

Mehemea ko Rupe!
If only I were Rupe!

Māui changed himself into a pigeon and flew to the uppermost heaven. Rupe is the name for a pigeon.

Evening
He ahiahi whatiwhati kāheru.
It is evening that breaks the spade.

As the day draws to a close the diggers work harder to get the job done.

Evil
He pirau kai mā te arero e kape.
The tongue rejects rotten food.

Similarly, evil is soon discovered, and put away.

E whai tonu mai te kino i a tātou.
Evil keeps on pursuing us for ever.

Evil, averting
Tūruki whakataha!
Go on one side and become powerless!

An exclamation in the form of a charm, ejaculated by anyone who has stumbled over a rock or a root. To do so was an evil omen, which could be avoided by this short charm.

Evil, origin of
Ko Whiro te pūtake o te kino o te ao.
Whiro is the root of evil in the world.

Whiro was the god of evil and darkness. He contended with Tāne in the search for the baskets of knowledge in the heavens and brought insects, bats and evil spirits to help him in the battle. Tāne drove him down to the lower worlds, where he continues to assail mankind with evil, sickness and death.

Example, bad
Kapo atu koe i te kai i ngā ringaringa o ngā pakeke, ā, taea rānei e koe te whai ngā tūranga o ō tūpuna?
You will snatch food from the hands of elderly people. Do you intend to follow in the footsteps of your ancestors?

Exasperation
Haere i a tuku noa, i a heke noa. Māu ka oti atu, oti atu.
Go your own silly way, but you will never return.

The free translation is from Elsdon Best. It is a whakamania or contemptuous or abusive form of address. It could almost be rendered 'Go to hell!'

Excess
Me he wai tā tieke.
Like the saddleback sprinkling itself with water.

Good in moderation, but one can have too much of a good thing.

Excuses
Kei kai i te ketekete.
Like disappointment over food.

Like greeting guests with regrets that food had not been prepared for them. Colenso puts it: 'Lest there be nothing to eat but vain regrets.' A chief would sometimes give this warning to his tribe when visitors were expected.

Kirikiri kai ota, he tangata ringaringa.
There are baskets of uncooked food, and we are men with hands.

Grey renders the proverb: 'Oh, never mind your large basket of food being uncooked; we are men and we have hands to cook it.' The saying was applied to someone who wanted to keep his provisions, and who made the excuse to visitors that he had no cooked food ready for them.

Experience
Ka motu te māhanga i te weka e kore a muri e hokia.
The woodhen escaped from the snare does not return.

Another form reads:
Makere te weka i te māhanga e hoki āno?

Yet another:
Hoki atu i konā, ko te manu i motu i te māhanga, e kore e taea te whai.
You had better go back, for it is useless to chase the bird that has escaped from the snare.

E hokihoki Kupe?
Will Kupe return?

After Kupe's discovery of New Zealand he returned to his homeland. The proverb has something of the same meaning as the previous one, the English equivalent of which is 'Once bitten, twice shy.'

'Tūraungatao e, e pēwhea ana te mamae?'
'Tāria iho. Kihai he hangahanga ake te kai a Tūraungatao.'
'O Tūraungatao, how is the pain?'
'Wait a while.' 'What Tūraungatao had was not sufficient.'

A young untried warrior is speaking to an old and experienced fighter before the battle. The old warrior tells him to wait, and then after the battle, when the young man has been wounded, he makes his final remark. Tūraungatao has been rendered as stand-against-a-hundred-spears.

Extinction
Mate ā moa.
Dead like the moa.

The gigantic bird of New Zealand has been dead for centuries, but at one time was hunted for food.

Another version, applied to a tribe, is:
Ka ngaro ā moa te iwi nei.
The tribe will be hidden, or disappear, like the moa.

Yet another:
Ko te huna i te moa.
Destroyed like the moa.

Ka oti te kakati i te kawau waha nui.
The big-throated shag has closed its beak firmly.

The fish has no hope once the shag has seized it.

Ko te heke rā o Maruiwi, i toremi ai ki te reinga.
Like the migrating Maruiwi, who all disappeared into the world of spirits.

It is said that the Maruiwi were travelling at night. They came to a deep chasm called Te Rehunga, which could not be seen in the dark, and one by one they walked into it and were killed.

Another shorter version:
Ko te waro a Te Rehunga.
This is the cavern of Te Rehunga. This is used as a warning.

Te umu ka pirau.
The oven whose fire is extinguished.

Applied to a tribe which has been completely exterminated.

Hāhā uri, hāhā tea.
Desolate darkness, desolate brightness.

Kōhere says: 'Come to nothing.'

Eyes
Me te Ōturu.
Like the full moon.

Radiant like the moon on the sixteenth night. Colenso says: 'Her eyes as large and brilliant as the full moon rising over the dark hills in a clear sky.'

Faint-heartedness
Ka mahi te take, paki ranga.
Well done, you are like a shallow-rooted tree.

Said ironically of one who is easily discouraged.

49

Fame
He toa taumata rau.
Bravery has many resting places.

The fame of a brave man is known to many.

He tini ngā whetū e ngaro i te kapua iti.
Many stars can be concealed by a small cloud.

Familiar places
Ko ōku kainga waewae.
The places my feet have trod.

Family, keeping troubles within the
E moe i tō tuahine, kia kino, e kino ana ki a koe anō.
Marry your cousin, so that if evil comes it will be kept to yourself.

In this saying tuahine means female cousin rather than sister. The thought behind it is that if there is a quarrel between man and wife it is far better that they should belong to the same family, for if they came from different whānau there was always a danger of intertribal warfare resulting.

Family quarrels
Ka mahi te tamariki wāwahi tahā!
Well done, children who break the calabashes!

A saying applied to a man who deliberately injures his relations, and is likened to mischievous children who break their parents' calabashes.

Fate
Haere. Mōu tai ata; mōku tai ahiahi.
Go your way. The morning tide is for you; the evening tide is for me.

A remark made by Tūmiromiro who consulted a flax leaf as an oracle and received an unfavourable omen.

E kore a Kiwi e mate. Mā Rehua i te rangi e kī iho kia mate a Kiwi, ā, ka mate.
Kiwi will not die. If Rehua in the sky says that Kiwi will die, only then will he die.

Kiwi Tāmaki was a famous chief of the Maungawhau (Mount Eden, Auckland) pā, who made this reply when his death was prophesied.

Fault-finding
He kūkū ki te kāinga, he kākā ki te haere.
A pigeon at home, a parrot abroad.

A person who doesn't dare to raise his voice in his own village and is as quiet as a pigeon, but when away from home finds fault with everything, and chatters like a parrot.

Faults
He kino tangata e kore e taea; he kino rākau ka taea.
It is impossible to deal with a bad man; but timber can be dealt with.

A human fault cannot be overcome; a fault in timber can be dealt with.

Favouritism
Māu anake te kai pai.
The good food is for you alone.

The saying is attributed to Manaia, who addressed these words of approval to his illegitimate son who rushed to his defence while his legitimate son drew back.

Feasting
Te hoa o te kai.
The friend of the feast.

Applied to one who is always found where food is being prepared and eaten.

Fernroot
Ka ora karikari aruhe, ka mate tāriki kākā.
Fernroot diggers enjoy good health, while parrot snarers die.

Fernroot or aruhe was the staple diet, obtainable all the year round, while other forest foods could be secured only in certain seasons.

Ferocity
Tangaroa kiriuka.
Unflinching Tangaroa.

Tangaroa was the god of fishes. Here, he may stand for the shark, a symbol of ferocity and courage.

Ngā pāniwhaniwha ngau pūraho a Te Aotauru.
The little snappers of Aotauru bite the lashings of the bait.

Aotauru was a notable, strong-minded woman whose descendants were known for their ferocity. Pāniwhaniwha is a small pink fish resembling a snapper.

Fertility
He poporo tū ki te hamuti.
A fruiting tree grows well on a dunghill.

Evidently a saying brought from the homeland. Poporo was the breadfruit tree of Hawaiki.

Fickleness
Ko te uri o Kōpū-manawa-whiti.
This is the offspring of Kōpū-manawa-whiti.

Applied to a person who changes his mind. The last part of the name can be rendered literally 'change of heart' with the same meaning in English and Māori.

Fighting
Te umanga a nehe mā he whawhai.
The occupation of ancient days was fighting.

Te umanga a nehe mā ko te whawhai.
The great occupation.

Anā te kai a Tama-tāhei ki a koe.
See, the food of Tama-tāhei for you!

A challenge made as a man thrusts with a weapon. Tama-tāhei was the name of a place noted for its mānuka trees, the timber of which was used to fashion weapons. If the thrust was successfully parried, the reply would be: *'Ehara, kei tua o Kapenga e haere ana.'* — 'Never! It has passed on the other side of Kapenga.' Kapenga was the name of a flax swamp, and Judge Smith conjectured that the 'buckler' with which the blow was parried might be of flax. Coarse flax cloth was sometimes wound round the arm for this purpose.

Finality
Ka tuwhaina te huare ki te whenua, e hoki atu rānei ki tōu waha?
If you spit on the ground, will the spittle return to your mouth?

A word of warning to those who do not think before they act, or look before they leap.

Nā wai te tara whai ka uru kei roto, e taea te whakahoki?
By whom can the barb of the stingray be removed once it has entered in?

Said by a chief who had stolen another's wife, when the husband demanded his wife's return.

Finding something lost
Kei te raumati ka kitea ai e koe ki te tupu.
Perhaps you will discover where it is by its shoots in the summer.

A saying for those who cannot be bothered to look for a lost article.

Kāore e hoatu e au, tā te mea ko te paekura kite a Māhina.
I will not give it up; it is the lost property which Māhina found.

Tauninihi had thrown his red feather hair ornament into the sea when the red pohutukawa blossoms were observed on the arrival of *Te Arawa* canoe. It was found by Māhina, who would not give it back.

Another version says:
He kura pae nā Māhina, e kore e whakahokia atu ki a koe.
It is the kura of Māhina which was cast ashore and cannot be returned to you.
See also Conclusion, false.

53

Finery
Ko ngā rangatira a te tau tītoki.
The chiefs of the tītoki season.

It is said that tītoki and tāwhara bear fruit every fourth year only. When that season comes round, tītoki oil is abundant and can be easily obtained. Commoners may then apply the oil mixed with red ochre, and give themselves the appearance of great chiefs.

Fire
Me oioi ki te ringa ka puta te tama a Ūpoko-roa.
When the hand is moved backwards and forwards, the child of Ūpoko-roa appears.

Ūpoko-roa, or Long-head, is the personification of comets. The reference to the hands moving is to the action of rubbing the firestick which kindles the flame. The child of Ūpoko-roa is therefore a figurative name for fire. Hare Hongi stated that Ūpoko-roa was a 'sarcastic allusion to fire'.

Firmness
E tia, me te wheke e pupuru ana.
It is as though in the grip of an octopus.

The analogy of the firm grip of an octopus is used of a weapon which penetrates an opponent's body and is difficult to withdraw.

A similar proverb is:
Mehemea kei te paru e titi ana.
As if it were sticking in the mud.

It is as difficult to pull my spear out of his body as if I had stuck it into tenacious mud.

Fishing
He kōrero taua ki Wharaurangi, he kōrero tā matau ki Ōtuawhaki.
The talk is all of war at Wharaurangi, but at Ōtuawhaki they speak of the making of fishhooks.

Wharaurangi is the hill above the famous rock Pōhaturoa, while Ōtuawhaki was a pā where fishing canoes were kept at the riverside. A contrast is made between the interests and conversation of warriors and fishermen.

Flight

He popotai numanga kino.
A banded rail disappears hurriedly.

A banded or land rail is a bird.

Kua riro ki wīwī, ki wāwā.
They have fled into the unknown.

Grey says that the saying is applied to crops which have failed, and to people who are not to be found where they were expected.
See Dispersal.

Flood

Te hurihanga i Mata-aho.
The overturning of Mata-aho.

An expression for flooded land. In the actual overturning performed by the god Mata-aho, Papa, mother earth, was turned on her face so that she should no longer grieve for her husband Rangi.

Followers

Ngā huruhuru o ōku waewae.
The hairs on my legs.

An expression used of the followers of an important chief; also of his renown. By changing the ōku to ōna, the saying is applied by men to their leader.

Food

Kei takahia a Tahu.
Lest Tahu be trampled on.

Do not slight Tahu. Tahu personified food supplies. The proverb is quoted when someone refuses hospitality. Tahu also appears in the phrase:
Ko Tahu kia rōria.
Let the tapu be removed from Tahu.

This is the whakarori ceremony which removes harmful influences from food and destroys tapu.

E hoa mā! Inā te ora o te tangata.
O friends! Here indeed is the health of mankind.

A statement made to a visitor when food is set before him.

He kino kai e kore e rere ki te pai tangata, he pai tangata ka rere ki te kino kai.
Bad food will not change a good man, but a good man will transform bad food.

The meaning seems to be that bad food will not demean a good man. He will dignify the food he eats, no matter how bad it is.

He whā tāwhara ki uta, he kiko tāmure ki tai.
The flowers of the kiekie on land, and the flesh of the snapper in the sea.

Good food is to be found everywhere. However, it may be that the proverb refers to food that is not greatly appreciated. Kōhere points out that tāwhara is the flower and not the fruit of the kiekie, and that the snapper was not greatly appreciated by the Māori unless it was eaten raw.

Food, cold
Ko ngā uri o Tūhourangi kai mātaotao.
The descendants of Tūhourangi eat cold food.

Grey explains that it was food which had been kept so long that it had grown cold.

Food, preservation of
Ka kitea a Matariki, na kua māoka te hinu.
When the Pleiades are seen, then the preserved flesh is cooked.

The flesh of birds, rats, and so on, was preserved in fat, the work being done in May or June when the Pleiades appeared.

Food, scarcity of
Ngā uri o Whaitiri whakapaparoa kai.
The descendants of Whaitiri who made food scarce.

This saying originates in the belief that when men of very high rank pay a visit, birds, fish and animals which provide food will leave their normal haunts for some time because of the mana of the visitors. Whaitiri drove fish away by her mana. The offspring of Whaitiri were her grandsons Tāwhaki and Karihi, who stole the blind woman's taro or kūmara roots.

From this incident arose another saying:
Ngā kai tatau a Whaitiri.
The counted food of Whaitiri.

The blind woman counted her taro roots carefully, and so food that is treasured is spoken of as the counted food of Whaitiri.

Ngahuru kai hāngai, kōanga kai anga kē.
At harvest time eating openly, in spring eating secretively.

Food is plentiful at the time of harvest, but in spring one eats little and in secrecy in order not to cause offence.

Ko Pūtauaki te kāinga he ngārara tāna kai.
Pūtauaki is the place where lizards are eaten.

Best says: 'If women . . . ate of the tuatara they would suffer for it, and probably perish, for they would be assailed by many lizards. So sayeth the Māori.'

Ko te kekerewai, ko te tuatara ngā kai o Wai-ō-hau.
Small green beetles and tuatara were the foods of the Wai-ō-hau district.

Food, sources of
He toka hāpuku ki te moana, he kaihua ki uta.
A rock in the sea where hāpuku abound, a tree where birds are speared on land.

Both are plentiful sources of food.

He tutu kākā kai uta, he toka kōura ki te moana.
A tutu bush on which parrots feed on land, a rock in the sea where crayfish gather.

Food staple
Te manawa nui o Whete.
The great heart of Whete.

Whete was an ancestor of the Tūhoe tribe, noted for his valorous deeds after he had sustained himself with a large meal of his favourite food, fernroot. The Tūhoe people therefore referred to fernroot by means of this expression. It has also been freely translated as: 'The sustaining power of Whete.'

Food supplies
Tiketike ngahuru, hakahaka raumati.
High in autumn, low in summer.

In autumn food is plentiful, in summer the supplies dwindle; or boasting in autumn when the crops are gathered, but in summer, when there is work to be done, he is absent.

Taku waha kai marangai ki roto o Maiaiti, taku waka tē toia, tē haumatia.
My mouth is always satisfied at Maiaiti, rough though the weather might be, where no canoe need be launched, nor is a voice heard to urge.

The translation, which is extremely free, is by Kōhere, who stated that this famous saying was uttered by the chief Tangi-tāheke. He was related both to Ngāti Porou and Whānau-a-Apanui, and when visiting them had learned how easily seafood could be obtained from a pool in the rocks at Maiaiti. Later, when caught by bad weather at Whakatāne and unable to catch fish, he longed for the plentiful supply of food at Maiaiti.

Foolhardiness
Haere ki Patiarero!
Go to Patiarero!

The saying comes from Wanganui, and it is said that the meaning is really: 'Go, so that they may eat you!' It is applied to one who insists on running into danger.

Haere i ngā ruruanga a Rangiwhenua.
Go with the brandishings of the thunder god.

Rangiwhenua was one of the gods of thunder. A headstrong person who goes into battle too impetuously is warned that he is rushing into the arms of danger.

I pāia koia te reinga?
Is the entrance to the spirit world blocked up?

This is said to one who is always attacking others, and likely to get himself killed prematurely.

Foresight
Kai mata whiwhia, māoa riro kē.
Uncooked food retained, cooked food confiscated by others.

Judge Smith says, 'Eaten underdone, you get it; fully cooked, somebody else may. A bird in the hand is worth two in the bush.'

Forest
Te wao tapu nui a Tāne.
The great sacred forest of Tāne.

Tāne was the god of fertility, and of the forest, which was sacred because he was its creator and guardian. Before a tree was cut down, propitiatory rites were offered to Tāne.

Forgetfulness
He taonga tonu te wareware.
Forgetfulness is an enduring property.

Forgetfulness, or thoughtlessness, is always with us.

Fortifications
He whare maihi e tū i te wao, he kai nā te ahi, he whare maihi e tū ki roto ki te pā tūwatawata koinā te tohu rangatira.
An ornamented house built in the wilderness is food for fire; but an ornamented house sheltered behind the stockade of a pā is the emblem of nobility.

Fortunes, changing

Waiho rā, e hika! He toi tipu te tangata, he toi heke.
Let it be, my friend! Man grows to a certain point and then descends.

A saying which refers to the varied fortunes of men, which wax and wane. It is a significant remark, made by a family when refusing the offer of marriage to a child or a young woman.

Ka pari te tai moana, ka timu te tai tangata.
As the tide of the ocean flows, the tide of man recedes.

A reply made by Te Rauparaha when his opponent Te Wherowhero said: *'Kei ahau te huka o te riri'* — 'I have retained the foam of battle.'

Freedom

Me he manu motu i te māhanga.
Like a bird escaped from the snare.

Haere ki wīwī, ki wāwā.
Go anywhere you like.

See Dispersal.

Friends, false

Hoa piri ngahuru, taha kē raumati.
Like a friend who sticks to you in autumn, but departs in summer.

Autumn is the time of harvest and plentiful food supplies, summer is the time of scarcity and hard work.

Frost

Ngā huka kokoti kōmata.
The frosts will cut down the young shoots.

Frugality

Te kete rukuruku a Whakaotirangi.
The little bundle in Whakaotirangi's basket.

Whakaotirangi was a woman of the Arawa canoe who hoarded a small quantity of seed kūmara in the corner of a basket. The saying is used when only a little food can be given to a guest.

There are several forms of the proverb. One is:
Ko te rukuruku a Whakaotirangi.
Gathered into the small compass of Whakaotirangi.

The basket is called both te kete rukuruku and te kete rokiroki.

Fruitless quest
Te whai papatu a Raupō-roa.
Long Bulrush kept on clashing.

Although the leaves of the raupō or bulrush rustle together in the wind and strike each other like weapons, it is all in vain, for they cannot be heard at a distance. So is a person who comes back to his own people without having achieved his purpose.

Futility
Ka tō te rā i a koe? He tupua, he tawhito te rā e tū iho nei.
Can you make the sun set? The sun standing up above is a supernatural being.

Gales
Ngā uaua o te whitu rāua ko te ono.
Strong as the sixth and seventh months.

The persistent equinoctial gales of early November.

Generosity
Tēnā te mana o Rehua.
Behold the greatness of Rehua.

Rehua was the god of kindness. The proverb is quoted by chiefs when making gifts.

Te uri o Māhanga whakarere kai, whakarere waka.
The offspring of Māhanga give away their food and their canoes.

Applied to generous, open-handed people.

Another proverb with the same theme is:
Te uri o Tūhoe moumou kai.
The offspring of Tūhoe give away (literally 'waste') their food.

61

Ko ana kai makamaka i aroha nei au; Ko te waka tē toia, tē haumatia.
It is his food so freely scattered about that I have at heart; his canoe dragged ashore without any voice to urge it.

The Ngāti Porou chief Whetū-kamokamo was noted for his generosity, and this saying was part of the lament composed for his death. As soon as the canoe appeared, everyone crowded on the beach. Whētu threw fish to everyone, and afterwards they all joined in pulling the canoe ashore without urging.

He kai titowera rawa hoki nāu te wai?
Is water a food that is prepared by cooking?

Or does water ever need to be cooked? The moral is that one should never begrudge small acts of kindness which make few demands on time or energy.

He iti kai mā tangata kotahi e kai, kia rangona ai te reka.
If there is only a little food, let only one eat it in order that its sweetness may be appreciated.

Gifts
Kia whakaoho koe i tāku moe, ko te whatutūrei a Rua.
Rouse me from my sleep only if you bring me some of Rua's cakes.

The whatutūrei of Rua were appetising cakes made from crushed hīnau berries.

In an alternative form:
Kia maranga ake aku kamo, ko te whatutūrei a Rua.
So that when I awake my eyes may rest on the jewel-treasure of Rua.

This translation is by Hare Hongi. Additionally, an interesting tale was told of the chief Matakore, as related by Leslie G. Kelly. Ngāti Matakore became a prosperous and powerful tribe. Their territory was fertile; the rivers teemed with eels; and forest foods abounded. Matakore, as befitting his rank, was the recipient of the first-fruits of the soil, the rivers and forests. Unlike other chiefs, Matakore was not particularly partial to animal foods and one day he was awakened from his noon-day rest to partake of a special repast of preserved birds. He scanned the fare placed before him with little interest, and presently he again composed himself for sleep. As he turned once more to his couch he was heard to murmur the following:

Kia whakaara ana koe i taku moe, ko te whatutūrei a Rua!
Would that you had disturbed my sleep for the much desired food of Rua (that is, the berries of the hīnau, actually however, the companionship of a beautiful woman).

Dr Bruce Biggs translates this as: 'If you waken me from sleep, let it be for the delicious food of woman.'

Ko te rourou iti a haere.
This is a little basket of food for the travellers.

Gluttony
Pāpaku a ringaringa, hōhonu a korokoro.
The hand is shallow but the throat is deep.

Said of a lazy person with a gluttonous appetite.

Hōhonu kakī, pāpaku uaua.
Deep throat but shallow (weak) muscles.

Āwhato ngongenga roa.
The caterpillar eats for a long time.

The glutton is like a caterpillar which never stops eating.

Ka kai kōpū, ka iri whata, kei te uaua te kore. Tōna kaha kei te kakī, karapetau tonu.
He fills his belly with food and rests at the food store, but his muscles are weak. His throat is strong from gulping down his food so greedily.

Ka mahi Tūhoropunga ki tāna mahi.
Tūhoropunga at her work was to be admired.

Tūhoropunga was noted for her gluttony.

Ko Uenuku tō korokoro!
Your throat is as powerful as Uenuku's!

A terse saying which literally means: 'Your throat is Uenuku.' Uenuku was an atua or god.

Tohu noa ana koe, e Rangi-kiato, he whata kei te kakī.
You are persistently storing away food, O Rangikiato.

Your throat is like a storehouse.
See also Greed.

Gods, all-seeing
Ko Tāne mata nui.
Tane has big eyes.

Grey says: 'Mind, therefore, what you do, for he is a god, and can see you, although you cannot see him.'

Gods, favour of
E nui e te whakahere, e tau e Tama-i-waho.
The larger the propitiatory offering, the more satisfied Tama-i-waho will be.

Kōhere says that Tama-i-waho was the sternest of the gods. He quotes a similar proverb:

E nui e te whāinga-ā-kai, e tau e Tama-i-waho.
The more plentiful is the heap of food, the more favourable is Tama-i-waho.

Gods, fickle
He atua huaki rangi, waiho te mate mō Hāpopo.
A god promised success through the priest Hāpopo, but death remained with Hāpopo.

He atua rere te atua, mahue raru a Hāpopo .
The god is a timid god, so Hāpopo was left in the lurch.

This translation by Kōhere.

Gods, liberality of
Kainga te tahua a Rongo rāua ko Haumia.
Eat the heap of food provided by Rongo and Haumia.

Rongo was the god of agriculture, Haumia the god of fernroot.

Gods, protection of
Ki a koe, e Maru. Māu e tiaki.
To you, o Maru. Protect me.

A prayer or appeal addressed to a tribal god in time of peril. Maru was a tribal atua. The speaker would of course appeal to the war god of his own tribe.

Good character
He whiro rānei koe, he ahurangi rānei?
Are you an evil person, or one of good character?

In certain rites in which a man was required to be purified, the tohunga would ask this question. The man could be relied upon to give himself a good character, but the priest would be sure to know whether he was an ahurangi, a worthy person of blameless character, or not.

Gordian knot
Kei te ruru tāku, te ruru a Te Ihonga.
My belongings are fastened together with the lashings of Te Ihonga.

Te Ihonga was a god or demigod who tied up a basket so that no one who did not know the secret of the knot could undo it.

Gossip
Tangaroa piri whare.
Tangaroa hides in the house.

Tangaroa was a god. The proverb is applied to an eavesdropper and gossip. An equivalent English proverb is 'Walls have ears.'

Greed
He kūkū tāngaengae nui, he pārera apu paru.
A pigeon with a big crop, a duck cramming mud into its beak.

Kai kino ana a Te Arahē.
The despicable eating habits of Te Arahē.

GREED

Te Arahē was a woman who ate the best food secretly, without sharing it with her husband.

Kōpaki tuhera, tū ana Tamaika.
When the basket is opened, Tamaika will be there.

Tamaika was an ancestor with an insatiable appetite for eels.

He kākā kai uta, he mangō kai moana.
A parrot feeding on land, a barracouta feeding in the sea.

Both the kākā and the barracouta are known for their voracity.

He kiore puku rua.
A rat with two stomachs.

A saying applied to a greedy person who is never satisfied.

He moumou kai mā Te Whataiwi puku ngakengake.
Food is wasted when given to Te Whataiwi of the distended belly.

Colenso remarks that two peculiar terms are to be noted here; one, the figurative name given to the person Whataiwi, that is, one who puts by dry bones, including fish heads, for himself on a platform for storing food; and two, the ludicrous term (not the common one) for big belly, that is, the loose-hanging bag of a large sea net!

Kei whaka Te Humu.
Do not make a Te Humu of yourself.

Te Humu lived near a large village. Whenever visitors arrived he quickly ran on to the marae and began to eat the food prepared for others. He was noted for his appetite on such occasions.

Āwhato kai paenga.
The caterpillar eats round the edges of the leaves.

The greedy person is likened to a caterpillar.

Ka mahi te āwhato hohoni paenga.
Well done, caterpillar nibbling the edges of the leaves.

An extended and more popular version of the previous proverb. It is applied to a greedy person who, having eaten his own basket of food, goes from one person to another taking something out of each basket.

He kākāriki kai ata.
A parakeet that eats early in the morning.

A greedy person begins to eat as soon as he gets up, instead of waiting until his work is done.

Patua iho, he kākā, ki tahaki tērā; titiro iho ka pūehuehu, mā tana whaiaro tēnaka.
Pound the food; if you find a stringy portion, put it on one side; but when you have a mealy piece, take it for yourself.

Fernroot had to be pounded on account of its stringy fibres.
See also Gluttony.

Grief
He wahine tangi tīkapa me he ngaru moana, taro ake kua paki.
A woman's mournful wailing will, like a wave of the sea, be calm again in a short time.

Grumbling
Tū te wheke, tū te mania.
The persistent grating and creaking.

Hair
Me rimurehia.
Like seagrass.

Rimurehia is a seaweed with long, shining strands.

Hair, grey
Ka tata ki a koe ngā taru o Tura.
The weeds of Tura are on you.

Tura was an explorer who married a woman of a strange race of people. While his wife was combing his hair she discovered his grey hairs and did not know what they portended, for her people did not die of old age.

Tura was aware that they were a sign of advancing age, and left his wife and child to return to his own people.

Hardihood

He atua te hiaora i te makariri.
A person who is like a supernatural being, because he is able to survive intense cold.

Hai aha mā te uri o Uruika?
What does it matter to a descendant of Uruika?

Uruika was an ancestor who travelled abroad in all weather.

Harvest

He kōanga tangata tahi, he ngahuru puta noa.
At digging time only one man will turn up; at harvest time there is no limit to the number of helpers.

Puanga kai rau.
Puanga of plentiful food.

When the star Rigel rises, food will be abundant.

Ko Whānui e! Ko Whānui!
Here is Whānui! Here is Whānui!

A cry raised by the first person to see the rising of Vega. It was not until Whānui appeared that the crop was ready to be lifted.

Kākāriki tunua, kākāriki otaina.
Parakeets cooked, parakeets raw.

A party of warriors on the war path has no time to be fussy about whether food is properly cooked or not.

Korikori tāua, ka taka tauira.
Let us two be moving, the sun is sinking.

Tauira usually means teacher, pupil or pattern, but in this case it is used figuratively for the sun.

Heart
He tānga kākaho koia kia kitea e te kanohi, tēnā ko te kokonga ngākau e kore e kitea.
If the reeds used in thatch are not straight, the eye can detect it; but the corners of the heart cannot be seen.

Any irregularity in the patterns of the reeds on the inside walls of a whare could be immediately detected.

A shortened version reads:
He tā kākaho e kitea, he tā ngākau e kore e kitea.
The crookedness of the reed is shown when the wind blows, the crookedness of the mind is not seen.

He kohonga whare e kitea, he kokonga ngākau e kore e kitea.
The corner of a house can be seen, but not a corner of the heart.

Heat
He koromiko te wahie e tāona ai te moa.
Koromiko wood was used to cook the moa.

Koromiko timber was burnt to heat the oven stones when moa flesh was cooked because it gave out an intense heat.

Kua tū te haka a Tānerore.
The dancing of Tānerore has begun.

Tānerore was the child of the summer maid and the sun. His haka or dance is the quivering, heated air of summer.

Heedlessness
Kapo rere te kurī.
The dog snatches and runs away.

Just as a dog snatches food from its master's hand and runs away without obeying him, so is a person who listens to another but takes no notice of what is said.

Heredity

E kore e taka te parapara a ōna tūpuna; tukua iho ki a ia.
He cannot fail to inherit the talents of his ancestors; they must descend to him.

He aha te ware noa ai? Nā Te Auripo.
Does it matter if he looks like a commoner? He is descended from the great chief Auripo.

Nāu i whatu te kākahu, he tāniko tāku.
The cloak is woven before the ornamental border is added.

It is the parents who are responsible for the character of the child.

E kore e hekeheke he kākano rangatira.
I will never be lost for I am of the seed of chiefs.

Our ancestors will never die for they live on in each of us.

Hero

Ko te tamaiti i tohia mō Tū.
This is the child who was dedicated to Tū.

Tū-mata-uenga, or Tū for short, was the god of war. Tohi was a baptismal ceremony in which boys were frequently dedicated to Tū; also a ceremony performed before or after a battle to make warriors invincible.

Holes

Mehemea i houhoua e te tieke.
Perhaps it was pecked at by a saddleback.

The saddleback is a bird that pecks at rotten wood in search of insects.

Home

Haere koe ki raro, ka mihi ki Pāmamaku.
Go north and you will sigh for Pāmamaku.

The southerners are proud of the fertility of their land, and the abundance of food to be found there.

Matua pou whare, rokohia ana; matua tangata, e kore e rokohia.
You can always gain shelter in your house, but not always with other people.

Even friends may die when you need them most.

Kia mau te tokanga nui a Noho.
Let the big basket be kept for Stay-at-home.

If you stay at home you will be regaled with large baskets of food, whereas the food supplies of travellers will be scanty.

Ko te tokanga nui ā Noho.
The big food basket of Stay-at-home.

Grey says that he who stays at home and minds his own business has abundance of food, while Colenso says: 'The peaceful dweller at home has always a thumping big basket of food to eat.'

Honesty
Waiho noa iho ngā tāonga, tēnā te mana o Tai-whanake.
You may leave your possessions in safety, for the influence of Tai-whanake is felt here.

An expression indicating that people at a certain place are honest and trustworthy.

Honour
Mō te oranga o te tama a Kiripuai, he kura te tangata.
The son of Kiripuai was saved from death because his father was held in such high esteem.

Hope
Iti noa ana, he pito mata.
Only an ordinary little morsel, but it has not been cooked.

If the uncooked morsel of kūmara is planted it will sprout, and there will be a harvest. Similarly, a warrior who escapes when his companions are killed may be the ancestor of many other warriors.

Hope, false
Te anga karaka, te anga koura, koi kitea ki te marae.
The husk of a karaka berry, the shell of a crayfish, should not be seen on the courtyard.

Lest they raise false hopes that a tempting meal is being prepared.

Hopelessness
Kore te hoe, kore te tātā.
No paddle, no bailer.

The saying is applied to a tribe which is hemmed in with no hope of escape from its enemies.

Ka kai a Koha i te kiko o tana ngarengare.
Koha must now make himself eat his own flesh.

Koha was besieged in his pā, Kohukete, and his people were starving and dying of thirst. As the chief saw the hopelessness of his position, he uttered these words.

Horizon
Te tāepaepatanga o te rangi.
The place where the sky hangs down to the horizon.

The expression refers to great distance, and open spaces.

Hospitality
Ko Maru kai atu, ko Maru kai mai, ka ngohengohe.
Maru who ate abroad, and at home, was agreeable.

Maru who fed those who entertained him was an agreeable and light-hearted fellow.

Kai ana mai koe he atua; noho atu ana ahau he tangata.
You are eating there like a god; I am sitting here as a man.

A warning against inhospitality. If a visitor arrives when one is eating, he should be asked to share the meal. If one neglects to do so, thinking that the unknown visitor is a person of low birth, he may prove to be a tohunga with power to wipe out the insult by death.

Hospitality of women
Te wahine a mea he aumiti tangata.
The wife of so-and-so gives a cordial welcome to a visitor.

Generosity and hospitality were highly esteemed in women. Mea is an expression meaning so-and-so or such-and-such a person if his name is not known.

Hunger
A, kua taka te tātua o Rangitaukē.
The belt of Rangitaukē slips down.

Poor Rangitaukē feels his belt slip down from his stomach because he is still hungry. A guest may offer this as a gentle hint that he would like more to eat.

Ngahuru kei runga, ngahuru kei raro.
Ten above, ten below.

A reference to teeth which are ready to bite any food no matter how hard or unpalatable, when a man is hungry.

Waiho i kona haere atu ai. Tēnā Te Hau-o-Puanui hai whakahoki mai.
Let her go. Te Hau-o-Puanui will bring her back.

A remark of Te Rangimonoa when his wife ran away. Te Rangi's friends urged him to follow her, but he knew that hunger would make her return. Te Hau-o-Puanui was the name of his foodstore.

Hunting
He manu kai kākano e mau, tēnā he manu kai rākau e kore e mau.
A bird which eats berries can be caught, but not a bird that eats wood.

Berry-eating birds are easily caught, compared with other species which eat wood or leaves.

Ka kai te kākā i te wai kaihua, ka kīia he rangi tahi.
When the parrots eat the honey of the rātā flower, then the birds will be plentiful.

When the rārangi tahi season arrives in January, that is, when the rātā is in full bloom and the birds begin to gather, the fowler puts his snares away and brings out his bird spears, for the birds will gather in such numbers that they can be taken easily.

Husband, hardworking
E moe i tangata ringa raupā.
Marry a man with blistered hands.

Husbandry
Kua tā noa ake te kōrau o Te Puku, tēnā ko tō Onea e kai tonu ana, e kore e hohoro te pau.
At Te Puku all the food has been consumed and only the young fern shoots are left, but at Onea food is still being eaten and it will not be exhausted quickly.

Hypocrisy
Ko te kōura kei te ūpoko te tūtae.
The crayfish has excrement in its head.

The crayfish makes itself out to be a fine fellow because its red clothing is like that of a chief, but its head is full of filth.

I tāia tō moko ki te aha?
Why have you got that tattoo design on you?

The thought is that the person spoken to has a good facial tattoo design, but he acts in a mean and cowardly fashion.

Identity, mistaken
Nā te pō a Wairaka i raru ai.
By darkness Wairaka was misled.

The chieftainess Wairaka was captivated by a handsome young man. When he lay down to sleep she noted his position in the whare and, when darkness fell, lay beside him and scratched his face so that he could be identified. But Mai-ure-nui, an ugly man, had changed places with her chosen man. When morning came Wairaka informed her father that her chosen husband could be identified by the scratches on his face. When Mai-ure-nui was revealed as her husband, the young woman uttered her plaintive cry.

Idlers
Maramara nui a mahi, ka riro i a noho.
The big chips of the workers are taken by those who are sitting down.

Grey capitalises mahi and noho, and renders the proverb: 'Mr Hardwork labours hard; Mr Sit-idly-by eats the food.' He says that while the workers laboured at hollowing a tree trunk to make a canoe, the idlers sat and watched but were eager to join in the meal that followed. Colenso puts it more succinctly, 'Worker (has) big chips gone with Squatter.'

Illegitimacy
He pōtiki na te koekoeā.
A child of the cuckoo.

Illegitimate children are likened to the young of the cuckoo, which are planted indiscriminately in the nests of other birds.

A similar proverb is:
Pēnei me te pīpī wharauroa.
Like the shining cuckoo.

Illness, recovery from
Māna anō e whakamāui ake.
He may rally again like Māui.

The saying is sometimes used of a person who is dying. Whakamāui is a verb meaning to recover from a severe illness, and originates in a legendary contest between Māui and the goddess of death in which Māui was defeated, but restored himself to life by chanting incantations. Subsequently Hine-nui-te-pō conquered him again and he died a final death.

Imitation
Whāia i muri i ngā waewae o Kōpū.
Follow in the footsteps of Kōpū.

Kōpū-manawa-whiti was a famous warrior. The saying is an incitement to act like a great chief.

Impatience
He tangata tunu huruhuru.
A hasty, quarrelsome man.

A proverbial expression which literally means one who roasts a bird without waiting to pluck the feathers.

Ka uia tonutia e koe, ka roa tonu te ara; ka kore koe e uiui, ka poto te ara.
The more you ask, the longer the way seems to be; the less you ask, the shorter your journey.

Ngā uri o Te Rangi-weka waewae wera.
The descendants of Te Rangi-weka who burnt their feet.

A proverb used of those who hurry on their way without staying to greet their friends.

Importance
He pōkeke Uenuku i tū ai.
Against a dark cloud the rainbow stands out brightly.

An important chief takes his place at the head of the tribe. Pōkeke is interpreted by Colenso as a dark cloud, and by Grey as thick misty rain.

Te ūpoko whakahirahira ko Rangitihi.
Rangitihi, the head of great importance.

Smith records it as 'Rangitihi, ūpoko whakahirahira' — 'Rangitihi, the arrogant, haughty-headed one.' But let us do justice to Rangitihi! Let us remember the other reference to his head in the entry Bravery.

He tangata anō te tangata ki tōna kāinga, ā, he ariki ki tōna iwi.
A man of importance in his own village, and a chief among his own people.

He ika paewai anake hei tomo i roto i te hīnaki.
Nothing but eels enter my eel pot.

There is a play on words in the proverb. Paewai is a species of eel, and ika paewai is a figurative expression for an important person.

Imposition

Kaua e hinga mai ki runga i a au, ka pā ia nā he urunga oneone ko te urunga mau tonu.
Do not lean on me as if I were a pillow made of earth that would remain firm.

Said to one who is always getting into difficulties and relying on his friends for help.

Impossibility

Me hīrau atu te rā koia, i haramia rā?
Can I pull the sun down with a forked stick, or prevent it from running its course?

Mā wai e rou ake te whetū i te rangi, ka taka kei raro.
Who can pull the stars down from the sky with a stick, so that they fall down here below?

The meaning appears to be that it is impossible to capture a powerful chief. This proverb is similar to the preceding one.

Inattention

Kei te kōrero mai ki tua o te hemihemi.
You are talking to the back of his head.

Inconstancy

Tūtohu ahiahi, whakarere hāpara.
Accept in the evening, reject in the morning.

Independence

He kai kei aku ringaringa.
I have food in my hands.

I can get food by using my own hands.

Ko Rauru tangata tahi.
Rauru, the man who stands alone.

Indestructibility

He puia taro nui, he ngata taniwha rau, e kore e ngaro.
Many taro roots in a clump, and hundreds of taniwha — these cannot be destroyed.

So it is impossible to completely exterminate a whole tribe. Colenso translates taniwha in this proverb as slugs or leeches.

Indigestion

He taua anō tā te kai.
Even food can attack.

Industry

Me whai anō au ki a Kāwai, ki te ringa tohau nui.
I will keep on following Kāwai, who is so industrious.

The speaker announces her intention of taking Kāwai for her husband. '*Ringa tohau nui*', literally big sweaty hand, is a figurative expression for an industrious person.

Tēnā te ringa tango parahia.
There is the hand that pulls up weeds.

Parahia is a small, low-spreading weed which would soon choke a kūmara plantation if it were not kept down.

Ko Kahungunu he tangata ahuwhenua mōhio ki te whakahaere i ngā mahi o uta me ō te tai.
Kahungunu is an industrious man who knows how to carry out work both on land and sea.

Me moe koe i a Tūrongo hei rangatira mōu, he tangata kaha ki te mahi kai.
You had better marry Tūrongo; he is a chief for you, a strong man in the procuring of food.

Tūrongo was a good bird hunter, and an expert in splitting logs for the building of houses.

Te whare huata a Māui.
Māui's house of spears.

The demigod Māui endeavoured to show his brothers the art of bird spearing. When Hotupuku, the taniwha of the Kaingaroa Plain, was killed, its stomach contained so many weapons that it was called '*Te whare huata a Māui*.' The proverb arose out of this incident.

He tangata whakaawe-kāpara.
A man of the planting season.

An expression for an industrious man.

Inevitability
Ka hia motunga o te weka i te māhanga?
How often does the weka keep on breaking away from the snare?

Sooner or later it will be caught.

Influence
He taumata, he whare nui.
A hilltop, a big house.

A hilltop can hold more people than the largest house. Similarly, a chief of elevated status gathers many supporters because of his influence.

Initiative
He kai ia nā tā te tou e hoake? Ka hua au me haere i muri o te tira parāoa.
Will sitting on your behinds bring you food? The only way to get what you want is to follow a great chief.

Parāoa is a whale, but the word is also applied figuratively to a chief.

Tū ana Raeroa, noho ana Raepoto.
Raeroa stands up, Raepoto sits down.

Mr Long shows initiative and gets what he wants; Mr Short is content to let fate take its course.

Innocent suffering
Kei uta te pakanga, kei tai te whiunga.
When inland tribes begin hostilities, the coastal tribes suffer.

Colenso renders it: 'Inland the fighting, at seaside the flinging.'

Integrity
E pango ana i waho, e mā ana i roto.
Black outside but white inside.

When a friend tried to dissuade Pōtatau from accepting the kingship of all the tribes, and said that he would be blackened in the eyes of men, Pōtatau replied, 'Yes, black without, but white within.'

He tangata kī tahi.
A man of a single word.

Taku kupu i whakaheia ki runga o Māramarama-te-rangi.
My word fulfilled in broad daylight.

Interference
He wahine te mea i pura ai te kanohi o Tahuaroa.
On account of a woman, Tahuaroa was blinded.

Tahuaroa had the misfortune to lose an eye because he intervened in a quarrel between a man and his wife.

Invincibility
He kotahi tangata, i a Whiti, i a Kahupeka, i a Te Rarokahaunga, ka tere te waka.
A single man, but there remain Whiti, Kahupeka and Te Rarokahaunga. The canoe floats.

The losses are small, for only one man has been killed. We still have notable fighting chiefs with us, and the canoe of our tribe still floats.

Kāore pea koutou e mōhio, ka tini, ka mano ki roto i a Wharepākau nei?
Do you not know that Wharepākau is equal to hundreds, to myriads?

A challenging statement of Wharepākau as he slew his foes single-handed.

Isolation
Ara te kōrero e piki rā i Tawhiti-a-Pawa, Takoto noa Waimahuru.
While news climbs over to Tawhiti-a-Pawa, Waimahuru is left isolated.

Tawhiti-a-Pawa was a steep hill between Waipiro and Tolaga Bay, over which a path climbed, while Waimahuru was a small, seldom-visited settlement below.

Jealousy
Ahakoa kai tahi, tērā a roto te hahae kē rā.
Although the meal is shared, jealousy is inside them.

The sharing of a meal is normally a sign of friendship, but the feelings of the heart go deeper than outward appearances.

Joyfulness
Kei te kamakama te tikanga.
It is a proper thing to be joyful and full of high spirits.

Smith renders the saying, 'Promptness carries the day.'

Kingship
Kotahi te kōhao o te ngira e kuhuna ai te miro mā, te miro pango, te miro whero. I muri, kia mau ki te aroha, ki te ture, me te whakapono.
There is but one eye of the needle through which the white, black and red threads must pass. After I am gone, hold fast to love, to the law, and to the religion of Christ.

The famous words spoken by Pōtatau Te Wherowhero, the first Māori King, at his coronation. He had been given the following charge by Te Heuheu: 'Pōtatau, this day I create you King of the Māori people. You and Queen Victoria shall be bound together as one. The religion of Christ shall be the mantle of your protection; the law shall be the whāriki mat for your feet, for ever and ever onward.'

Labour, satisfaction in
Ehara tā te tangata kai, he kai tītongi kau; engari mahi ai ia ki te whenua tino kai, tino mākona.
Food provided by someone else is only food to be nibbled; food produced by one's own labour on the land is good, satisfying food.

A more succinct saying with the same meaning is:
Tino kai, tino ora te kōpū.
Good food, good health for the belly. There are several other versions.

Land

Te toto o te tangata, he kai; te oranga o te tangata, he whenua.
Food supplies the blood of man; his welfare depends on the land.

Toitū he kāinga, whatu nga-rongaro he tangata.
The land still remains when the people have disappeared.

Māu te wahine, māku te whenua, kia ai koe i te tore tangata, kia ai hoki au i te tore whenua.
To you the woman, to me the land, that you may breed men while I grow food.

The proverb is concerned with the division of work between men and women.

Land, affection for

Tukua mai he kapunga oneone ki a au hai tangi.
Send me a handful of soil that I may weep over it.

A chief, taken prisoner in battle and condemned to slavery, made this request.

Land of peace and plenty

Ka kata ngā pūriri o Taiāmai.
The pūriri trees of Taiāmai are laughing.

Taiāmai is an ancient name for the fertile distict inland from the Bay of Islands. The saying symbolises the joy that comes from good news, as well as the beauty and perfection of nature, and is a term of honour addressed to a welcome guest.

Land, the permanence of

He kura tangata e kore e rokohanga, he kura whenua ka rokohanga.
The treasured possessions of men are intangible; the treasures of the land are tangible.

In a world where men and women and their possessions have no permanence, the land remains as the one possession which never changes nor is ever destroyed.

A similar proverb:
He kura kāinga e hokia; he kura tangata e kore e hokia.
The treasure of land will persist; human possessions will not.

Laughter
Ka kata Kae.
Kae is laughing.

Kae was the tohunga who stole Tinirau's whale. Tinirau sent a party of young women from village to village in search of the tohunga. The only way they could recognise him was by his deformed teeth. When they reached Kae's village the tohunga kept his mouth closed, but the young women sang a song which made him laugh and in this way he was discovered by his gapped teeth. 'Then the flesh of Tutunui was still to be seen in his teeth — his teeth which overlapped each other.' G. Powell says that when a man hears the amusing words of another, he says to him, *'Ka kata Kae'* in appreciation of the other's witticism. One can imagine the Māori expression meaning, 'It's enough to make Kae laugh!', much as we refer to making a cat laugh.

Laziness
Ko tūranga o Pōtaka.
The tiredness of Pōtaka.

A pointed remark made about lazy people. Pōtaka had the reputation of remaining on his sleeping mat while others were working. The form of the proverb is given by Taylor, but a more usual construction would be *'Te tūranga o Tūranga.'*

I whea koe i te tahuritanga o te rau o te kōtukutuku?
Where were you when the fuchsia began to put on its leaves?

A reproach against those who have absented themselves from the plantations during the planting season.

I hea koe i te tangihanga o te riroriro?
Where were you when the grey warbler was singing?

The song of the riroriro is heard in spring, and is the signal for planting to begin. Anyone who has been lazy at planting time and grumbles because he is hungry in winter is mocked with this phrase.

LAZINESS

He kai koutou ka hohoro, ko te ngaki e kore.
You are quick to eat, but not to work in the plantation.

Tū kē raumati, whakapiri ngahuru.
You keep well away in summer, but stick close in the autumn.

A lazy person is conspicuous by his absence when work has to be done, but is well to the fore when the food is ready.

Take kōanga, whakapiri ngahuru.
Absent at planting time, close by at harvest.

He kurī tahutahu, me te tangata he hiore tahutahu.
A man like a dog who sticks so close to the fire that he keeps on setting his tail on fire.

A shorter version:
He hiore tahutahu.
A frequently singed tail.

He kai ko tāu e pahure; ko te mahi, e kore e pahure.
At eating you accomplish much; at working, nothing.

He tangata kumu.
A man sitting on his behind.

A man who sits still and makes excuses for not working.

Kei uta ngā hau o Rīrapa e tū ai.
It is on shore that Rīrapa's spoils are gained.

Rīrapa would never accompany the fishermen but stayed ashore. When the fish were brought to the village he was in front of all the others at meal times.

Ngā huhunu, ngā wera tō kai, e māngere!
Burns and scalds are your food, lazybones!

A person who sits idly by the fire.

Leadership

Haere, e whai i ngā waewae o Rehua.
Go and follow in the footsteps of Rehua.

If one follows a great chief, such as Rehua, one can be certain of good food and entertainment.

Waiho rā kia tū takitahi ana ngā whetū o te rangi.
Let it be one alone that stands among the other stars in the sky.

Rākai-hikuroa's plea for a single leader for his people.

Heoi anō te whetū e tū nei, kotahi.
There is only one star standing there, and one alone.

Applied to the famous fighting chief of Tainui, Kāwharu, shortly before he was killed.

Legs

Ka mahi te waewae, i tōia i te ata hāpara!
How beautiful are the legs moistened in the dawn!

Grey's rendering: 'Well done, what pretty legs; they are so straight that one would think that when you were a baby, your mother must have amused herself in the morning's dawn, by sitting and rubbing them with water.' The limbs of babies were massaged to make them supple and shapely'.

Lies

Tapahia tō arero pēnei me tō te kōkō.
Cut your tongue as the tui's tongue is cut.

A sharp rebuke made to one who is detected in a lie. Kōkō is another name for the tui, which was sometimes kept captive, its tongue slit, and taught to talk.

Ko kōrua pea ko Tama-arero i haere mai.
Perhaps you and Tama-arero came here together.

Tama-arero is literally tongue's son, or man tongue, which Grey paraphrases as Mr Lying-tongue, and Colenso as False-tongue. The name Te Arahori or False-road is used in a similar proverb.

Different tribes had variants of these proverbs, another name which might well have come from *Pilgrim's Progress*, being:
Tango-kōrero.
Take-up-talk.

Arero rua.
Two-tongued.

One who cannot be relied upon to speak the truth.

A similar expression is:
Ngākau rua.
Two minds.

He arero rua.
A double tongue.

An epithet for a liar.

Te waha hakirara.
A lying mouth.

He paraki waha, he hāwatewate.
A dribbling mouth, a liar.

Life and death
Kei raro te whare o aituā, e hāmama i runga ko te whare o te ora.
The house of misfortune is below, gaping open above is the house of life.

A very early saying. Tāne and other gods sought long for the female element, which was eventually discovered in the earth. The female element or organ is the house of misfortune and death, while the abode of life is above in the sky. When Tāne asked Rangi where the female element might be found, Rangi's reply was given in the words of the proverb.

Ka mate he tētē, ka tupu he tētē.
As one frond dies another grows in its place.

Tētē is here used figuratively for a chief.

Listlessness
E noho kohiwi noa iho ana te tangata.
Nothing but the body of the man remains.

Applied to those who are indifferent, listless, enervated, or absent-minded.

Loneliness
Ko te uri o pani.
An expression used of one who has no family or friends, and therefore has no influence.

Me aha hoki ngā uri o Punga aruaru kai?
What can be done for the descendants of Punga, who chased his food?

Punga was the personification of lizards. His name was almost a synonym for ugliness.

Longing
Māu anō te tinana, māku te ata o te tāpara kau atu e.
For you the reality, for me only the shadow of desire.

He manako te kōura i kore ai.
There are no crayfish because you set your heart on them.

When they are expected, no crayfish are to be found. A warning against wishful thinking.

He mate kāhu korako.
Desire for the hawk with white feathers.

A kāhu korako, or light-coloured hawk, was a rare sight, and was a figurative expression for a chief. The saying is directed more particularly to a taurekareka or slave who has fallen in love with the daughter of a chief, and has no hope of his love being requited.

Looks not important
He kino rā, he kino nō tau o te wai.
I may not be good-looking, but I am the deepest part of the river.

LOSS

Said by Putaanga when disparaging remarks were made upon his appearance by Tamahae. Tau o te wai is the deep part of the river below the rapids where the largest eels lurk. Tau also means to adorn or make comely, and there may be a play on the meaning of this word.

Loss
Tō ngaki kai, te Tangaroa-meke, kei uta, kei tai te pakanga.
Whilst war rages on land and sea, you plant the food supplies of Tangaroa-meke.

The meaning is that though one may plant, changes will come and another who is victorious will reap the harvest.

Love
E iti noa ana, nā te aroha.
A small ordinary thing, begotten by love.

Although the present is small, it is all love has to give. A free translation.

Taku hei piripiri,
Taku hei mokimoki,
Taku hei tawhiri,
Taku kati taramea.
My pendant of scented fern,
My pendant of sweet scented fern,
My pendant of scented gum,
My sachet of sweet scented speargrass.

A form of endearment to a small child.

Aroha mai, aroha atu.
Love toward us, love going out from us.

Love received demands love returned.

Ko Hinemoa, ko au.
As for Hinemoa, as for me.

Grey puts it, 'I am just like Hine-moa; I'd risk all for love.'

Hinemoa was the young woman who left her own people and swam across Rotorua to the island of Mokoia, where her lover Tūtānekai waited for her.

Love, unrequited
Tō kahawai ngako nui aroaro tahuri kē.
Many plump kahawai are hauled up, but you turn your face away.

The young woman accepts gifts from her lover, but does not respond to his love.

Magic
Ngā uri o Kiki whakamaroke rākau.
The descendants of Kiki who caused trees to wither.

Applied to sorcerers or tohunga mākutu. Kiki was a famous sorcerer of the Waikato district.

Mana
Ko te mana i a Kārewa tōu mana.
You are as powerful as Kārewa, with all his influence.

Mana is a word with many shades of meaning — power, influence, prestige. It has become a part of the English language in New Zealand.

Mankind, common origin of
Nā Rangi tāua, nā Tū-ā-nuku e takoto nei; ko ahau tēnei, ko mea a mea.
You and I are both from the sky father and earth mother; this is me, so-and-so, son of such-and-such.

When strangers arrive at a village, the chief of that place says: 'Welcome! From whom are you descended?' The leader of the visitors replies in the words given above, referring to their common ancestry in Rangi, the sky father, and Papa-tū-ā-nuku, the earth mother, before giving his name and lineage.

Māoritanga
E tipu, e rea, mō ngā rā o tōu ao; ko tō ringa ki ngā rākau a te Pākehā hei ara mō tō tinana, ko tō ngākau ki ngā tāonga a ō tūpuna Māori hei tikitiki mō tō māhuna; ko tō wairua ki tō atua, nāna nei ngā mea katoa.
Grow up and thrive for the days destined to you, your hand to the tools of the Pākehā to provide physical sustenance, your heart to the

treasures of your Māori ancestors as a diadem for your brow, your soul to your God, to whom all things belong.

This is probably the most quoted proverb of the last forty years. It was written by the late Sir Apirana Ngata in the autograph book of one of the daughters of Sir John Bennett.

E kore e piri te uku ki te rino.
Clay will not cling to iron.

The proverb comes from the famous haka 'Mangumangu Taipō', composed in Taranaki. Wet clay clings to iron but as soon as it dries it falls off. Similarly, the Māori must take pride in his ancient culture, because Western accretions will eventually fall off, and the Māoritanga will remain.

Toi te kupu, toi te mana, toi te whenua.
The permanence of the language, prestige and land.

The words spoken by the chief Tinirau of Wanganui, the translation by the Reverend Kīngi Īhaka. Toi means origin, summit, native, and also art and knowledge, and the use of the word in the proverb is related to all these meanings. Īhaka says that the proverb stresses the fact that without the Māori language, without prestige or mana, and without land, Māoritanga will cease to exist.

Marriage
He hono tangata e kore e motu; kā pā he taura waka e motu.
A human bond cannot be severed; unlike a canoe rope, it cannot be severed.

Betrothal and marriage are permanent, unlike the mooring rope of a canoe, which can easily be broken.

Honoa te pito mata ki te pito maoa.
Join the raw end to that which is cooked.

Grey says that the proverb refers to a union of a rangatira and a woman of low birth. Chiefs frequently married slaves. Colenso draws another moral, 'Don't be too nice!'

Tāne rou kākahi ka moea, tāne moe i roto i te whare, kurua te takataka.
The man who gathers shellfish will be happily married; the man who spends all his time sleeping in the house will be struck on the head.

Women will commend husbands who are hard workers, but will not tolerate lazy ones.

He iti kōpua wai, ka hē tō manawa.
A small deep pool of water will exhaust the breath.

A saying quoted to a girl who wishes to marry at too early an age. Best translates it as 'A small pool of water will exhaust a man's breath if he immerses himself therein.'

Maturity
Taute te tītoki, whero te rātā i te waru.
The tītoki ripens its fruit, the rātā is red in the eighth month.

Memories
He kitenga kanohi, he hokinga whakaaro.
To see a face is to stir the memory.

People unfamiliar with Māori custom wonder why tears are shed so openly when there appears to be no apparent reason for so doing. Two people, men or women, spend some time greeting each other and it is because both have memories of each other, or someone known to both, that they spend so long greeting each other.

Mercy
Homai te kāeaea kia toro-māhangatia, ko te kāhu te whakaora, waiho kia rere ana.
As for the bush hawk, let it be caught in the snare, but spare the life of the harrier, so that it may fly once more.

The kāeaea or bush hawk is a symbol of a treacherous and cruel person, the kāhu or harrier that of a noble chief.

Waiho mā te whakamā e patu. Waiho hai kōrero i a tātau kia atawhai ki te iwi.
Let shame be their punishment. Let the talk of the people make us appear of a kindly disposition.

A famous saying attributed to an even more famous tohunga, Te Tahi-o-te-rangi. He had been marooned on White Island, but by means of his magic powers he escaped on the back of a whale. As he passed the canoes of those who had marooned him, the whale wished to overturn them, but Te Tahi spoke these pregnant words.

Messenger

Ko te uri o Te Paki-wae-tahi.
This is a descendant of Te Paki the single-footed.

Te Paki was an ancestor of Waikato who achieved his nickname because of his turn of speed.

Might

E kore e hohoro te opeope o te otaota.
The litter will not be swept up quickly.

The saying refers to a large war party which will not easily be defeated.

Ngā Puhi taniwha rau, Ngā Puhi kōwhao rau.
The many taniwha of Ngā Puhi, the many holes of Ngā Puhi.

Grey explains that the Ngā Puhi tribe is dangerous, for they have a hundred villages in which their warriors may assemble; whereas Kōhere says that the meaning is that the Ngā Puhi tribe is not united, because each hapu is self-supporting. Taniwha are fierce monsters, symbolising fighting chiefs, and kōwhao are holes, here used figuratively for fortresses.

Misery

Whanātu poho ki roto, haere mai tāiki ki waho, nohoia te whare, o te hē tonu.
The pit of the stomach falls in; the ribs stick out from sitting in the house; all has gone wrong.

Colenso observes that 'this is a highly ludicrous proverb; the joke, or point, being largely increased through the play on the three verbs — to recede, to come hither, and to squat idly indoors; or, increased as it is in the passive, to remain within to support the house!' It is used in times of cold and hunger, showing their effects. 'Too cold to go out, too hungry to remain indoors without food yet keeping house!, squatting idly, doing nothing.'

Misfortune

Tēnei tangata nui, a Aituā.
This overpowering person, Misfortune.

Evil and ill-fortune are personified in the term Aituā.

E hara ana te poporoihewa, e noho ana te kiore.
Although the whitehead goes away, the rat remains.

The whitehead is a forest bird. The rat personifies misfortune.

He tao huata e taea te karo, he tao nā aituā e kore.
The thrust of a war spear may be parried, but not the spear of misfortune.

Mismanagement

Na takaroa, na takahē.
Because of delays, things come to nothing.

Difficulties arise through delays and mismanagement.

Modesty

Waiho mā te tangata e mihi.
Let someone else acknowledge your virtues.

Kāore te kūmara e kōrero mō tōna māngaro.
The kūmara does not say how sweet it is.

Self-praise is no recommendation.

Moon

Kua mate te marama.
The moon is dead.

A reference to the waning of the moon, made with the knowledge that it will be reborn in the Waiora-a-Tāne, the lifegiving waters of Tāne.

Mother love

He aroha whāereere, he pōtiki piri poho.
A mother's love, a breast-clinging child.

Mourning

Wahine tangi haehae he ngaru moana, e kore e mātaki.
Wailing and laceration of women in mourning, like a wave of the sea, go on unceasingly.

Māori women gashed themselves with obsidian during mourning until they bled. Charcoal was often rubbed into the wounds to make an indelible record of all those they had mourned. The custom was called haehae.

He mate tino tangata, tēnā e renga mai.
When a great chief dies mourners flood in for the tangi (or mourning period).

Kāti te tangi, āpōpō tātau ka tangi ano, ā pā ko te tangi i te tai, e tangi roa, e ngunguru tonu.
Cease crying, tomorrow we shall mourn again. We are not like the sea, which is forever murmuring and rumbling.

This saying is quoted at a tangi when the wailing is prolonged.

Ka whati rā ia taku mahuri tōtara.
My tōtara sapling so suddenly broken off.

Said by a mother of a son who has died, as she grieves for him. The expression '*taku mahuri tōtara*' is one of great affection.

Waiho kia tangi ahau ki taku tūpāpaku; ā pā he uru tī e pihi ake.
Let me weep for my dead; he is not like the head of a cabbage tree that springs up again.

The tī or cabbage tree is noted for the way it grows again from a severed stump.

Another form of the saying is:
Ehara i te tī e wana ake.
Not like a cabbage tree which sends up a new shoot.

Murder

Ko Te Ngako ringa kino
Like Te Ngako of the evil hand.

Grey was of the opinion that this was a warning against waging war against Te Ngako's descendants, because their ancestor had a 'murderous hand'.

He patunga take kore, he tino kōhuru.
Killing without reason is truly murder.

Te kokonga pōuri.
The dark corner.

Murder is an evil deed performed in secrecy.

Purapura ora.
The seed of life.

A proverbial expression for the children of one who has been murdered.

Neatness
Me he toroa ngunungunu.
Like an albatross with its head nestled under its wing.

Contracted into a small space. The expression is applied to mats and garments which have been neatly folded.

Neglect
Ka rūhā te kupenga, ka pae kei te ākau.
When a net is worn out, it is thrown away on the shore.

The saying was used by an old wife complaining that her husband was neglecting her for a younger wife.

Tītī kainga tahi.
The muttonbird fed only once.

The muttonbird returns to feed its young only once a day. The proverb is used of a tribe which is not generous with food for visitors.

Nā wai i kī kia purua tētahi kōwhao, kia whakatuwheratia tētahi?
Who said that one hole should be stopped up, and another opened?

Ngā Tokorima, a Tūhoe chief, was overlooked when a tribute of birds was being distributed, and uttered these words. Best says that a kōwhao was a hole through which the lashing of the topstrake of a canoe was passed. Afterwards the holes were blocked up to prevent water entering the canoe. In a slightly different form the proverb goes: *Nā wai i kī tētahi kōwhao kia purupuru, tētahi kia whakatuwhera?*

Nephew
He irāmutu tū kē mai i tarawāhi o te awa.
A nephew stands on the bank of the river.

Instead of crossing the river to help, a nephew will stand on the far bank while you are being killed. The inference is that nephews cannot be depended on like sons. Shortland uses the proverb as an illustration of the custom that children of a female married to a man of another tribe have no right of succession to land in their mother's tribe.

New start
Tūngia te ururua kia tupu whakaritorito te tupu o te harakeke.
Set the overgrown bush alight, and the new flax shoots will spring up.

Clear away what is bad and the good will flourish. Īhaka said a fair interpretation of this is, 'Burn or dispose of whatever hinders progress in all that is done, in order that what is desirable may indeed grow and bear fruit.'

New year
Matariki ahunga nui.
The Pleiades with many mounds heaped up.

The new year was indicated by the appearance of the Pleiades or Matariki. The mounds were heaped up for the kūmara tubers, because the planting season was not far off. The following proverbs also indicate the importance attached to the rising of the Pleiades during winter, when thought must be given to the coming planting season. It was often a time of hunger, when food supplies were getting low.

Matariki hunga nui.
The time when people assemble.

The workers are gathering together.

News
Patua i tahatū o te rangi, waiho tangata haere wā kia haere ana, kia rongo ai koe i te kōrero.
When you strike, strike at the horizon. Leave the traveller to continue on his way, and then you will hear news.

News, out of date
Ka whaka Te Aropiri.
Behaving like Te Aropiri.

Te Aropiri had the reputation of telling people what they already knew.

Night
E kore e kitea te tui i ngā toke i te pōuri.
We cannot see how to thread worms in the dark.

When darkness comes it is time to leave off work. Worms were threaded as a bait to catch eels.

He tītī rere ao ka kitea, he tītī rere pō e kore e kitea.
The muttonbird which flies by day is seen, but the muttonbird that flies at night cannot be detected.

Showing the advantages of a night attack; also applied to men's thoughts.

Pekapeka rere ahiahi, hokioi rere pō.
A bat flies in the twilight, a hokioi by night.

The hokioi was a mythical bird which was never seen, but whose cry was heard in the darkness, and was greatly feared. Duff identifies it with the extinct giant eagle *Harpagornis moorei*.

Tiketike ao, pāpaku pō.
High during the day, low at night.

Boasting in the daylight, but scared in the dark.

Nobility

He purapura i ruia mai i Rangiātea.
The seed scattered abroad from Rangiātea.

Rangiātea was the homeland of the race where the famous marae Taputapuatea was located at Opoa. Rangiātea was also the temple in the twelfth overworld.

Kua whati te tihi o Tongariro.
The peak of Tongariro has been broken off.

A saying which indicated that a warrior was of exalted rank, but had not been tested in battle. It was said of Te Popo by Te Heuheu.

Noise

Ko te ahi tawa hai whakarite.
It can be compared to a tawa fire.

A saying about a noisy child. Ahi tawa is a fire at which tawa kernels are roasted, and is a term expressing noisiness. When the kernels are heated they make a popping sound.

North versus south

E raro rawa kore;
E runga tini hanga.
Those of the north are destitute;
the people of the south are well off.

Grey translates the proverb in the sense that the northern tribes are stupid, while the southerners have plenty to say and are learned in their traditions. Somewhat surprisingly, Colenso says the proverb originated in the north. He explained that material for the most treasured possessions — greenstone for adzes, weapons and ornaments, flax for the best garments, tōtara timber for canoes, and the feathers of the huia, all came from the southern parts of the land, and therefore the most skilled carvers and weavers were of southern origin, and were sometimes taken prisoner because of their skill.

Northern tribes

E kore te pakiaka hinahina e toro i runga i a au, e rongo ake au e 'mara' ana, e 'kihi' ana.

The roots of the hinahina tree would not creep across me before I would hear the language of Māori from the north, and of white men.

A prophecy made by Rangitauātia of Ngāti Porou. '*E mara*', meaning friend, is a term of greeting used by the Ngā Puhi and '*kihi*' is the 'kissing' language of the north, full of sibilants.

Now or never

Ka kore atu anō i Waitāia-iti, ā, i Waitāia-rahi.

Nothing at Little Waitāia, nor at Big Waitāia.

As no fish were caught at Waitāia-iti, a fisherman tried Waitāia-rahi, and was equally unsuccessful. A person who is promised something in the future quotes the proverb in the sense of 'A bird in the hand is worth two in the bush.'

Nuisance

Hei a au tonu koe waru ai?

Would you keep on scraping me?

Tīnātoka, the son of Tū-whakairi-ora, made a large kūmara pit and kept asking his neighbour Mahara for kūmara to fill it. After many applications Mahara grew tired of Tīnātoka's constant requests, and when the chief again approached him with an empty basket, he asked this question.

Numbers

I muia Tinirau i mate ai.

Because he was overwhelmed by numbers, Tinirau was killed.

Tini whetū ki te rangi, ko Ngāti Maru ki te whenua.

As the multitude of stars in the sky, so are the people of the Ngāti Maru tribe in the land.

Tau ana te āhuru o Pakarau.

Warm continues to rest on Pakarau.

Pakarau was a district occupied by a chief who had so many followers that no one dared attack him.

Obesity
He nui tangata nā te kai i whāngai.
A fat man has been nourished by food.

Probably said contemptuously, as obesity was not admired.

He kōkō kai kohe.
Like a tui which eats kohe.

Kōkō is a name for the tui or parson-bird, and the kohe is a berry-bearing tree. Tui which fed on a prolific tree got very fat, and the remark is a jesting one applied to fat people.

Obstacles
E Kauri e! Kua whati ngā toki. Waiho rā kia whati ana, e whati ana ki mahi rau a tama a Tāwake.
O Kauri! These adzes are broken. Let them break. They are broken in the many tasks of the son of Tāwake.

Tamatea-ure-haea and his men began to dig a channel to divert the Kaitāia Stream over their land, but the task was never finished because of the obstructions on which their tools were broken.

Obstinacy
Kia whakatupu tangata, kaua hei tutū.
Behave like a man; do not be obstinate.

This saying is often quoted to young people to encourage them to be obedient and to have a sense of responsibility.

Nā wai te kōau ka ruku ki te aromaunga e peka.
The shag that dives towards the face of the mountain will not be turned aside.

Kōau is another form of kawau, or shag. According to legend, a shag which flies up a narrow valley cannot be turned back.

Obstruction
He kōwhatu koe.
You are a rock.

Are you a rock that you won't get out of the way? Also applied to an obstinate person.

He ngārara whakapae huarahi.
A reptile that lies across the road.

The expression is used for any inadvertent hold-ups, particularly when calling into a marae to pay one's respects at a tangi because one has noticed that there is such an occasion in progress when one is travelling. Even if one does not know the corpse or the people, it is impolite, discourteous, to pass by without commiserating with the bereaved. It is on such occasions that this proverb is employed.

Offerings
E Maru! Ina tāu.
O Maru! Here is yours.

Maru was a tribal god of great power. A bird hunter would take the first bird he caught and throw it aside, using these words, by which he dedicated it to Maru.

Old age
Nā wai te kōkōmuka tū tara-ā-whare i kīia kia haere?
Now who said that the shrub which grows on the wall of the house should go abroad?

Kōkōmuka is the veronica, and the phrase '*kōkōmuka tū tara-ā-whare*' is a figurative one for a stay-at-home. The saying was repeated by old men when they were asked to take part in an expedition.

E maha ngā rangi ka tautau te remu ka taikuiatia ki te whare.
When you get old, your wrinkles will hang down, and you will loiter about the house like an old woman — do not, therefore, now despise old age.

He pakaru ā waka e taea te raupine mai.
A broken canoe can be repaired.

But when old age damages the body, youth and beauty cannot be restored.

Māku tēnei, mā te rā e tō ana. He aha kei a koe, kei te rā e huru ake ana?
Leave this for me, for the setting sun. What purpose does it have for the rising sun?

Such trifles should be left for the aged, because young people with their whole lives before them have no need of them. Colenso says that care for old people was an admirable trait in young people, and that he knew of no case in which the proverb was quoted and not responded to.

Omens
Kaua e patu aruhe i te pō; he ūpoko tangata, he tohu aitua.
Do not pound fernroot at night; a human head, a sign of evil omen.

As the saying shows, it is unlucky to pound fernroot at night. To do so is symbolic of having one's head beaten by the club of an enemy.

He maroro kokoti ihu waka.
A flying-fish that cuts across the bow of a canoe.

When a war party was on the march, the first person who crossed its path was killed, even though he might be related to someone in the taua. The unfortunate person was compared to a flying-fish cut off by the bow of a canoe.

Omniscience
Tangaroa pūkanohi nui.
Big-eyed Tangaroa.

The god of the sea can observe all we are doing.

Opportunism
He hūanga ki matiti, he tama ki tokerau.
A relative in the summer, a son in autumn.

There is work to be done in summer, so he only claims to be a distant relative, but in autumn, when food is plentiful, he claims to be a son.

Opposition
E kore koe e puta i ngā toretore o Waihī.
You will not pass through the rough seas of Waihī.

A warning against starting an enterprise which cannot be carried to a conclusion. Waihī is at the mouth of the Wairoa River where it runs into Kaipara Harbour, and at this point there is usually a high sea running.

Oratory
He kākā waha nui.
A loud-mouthed parrot.

This proverb is used of the eloquent orator who knows how to project his voice.

Organisations
He pō tūtata, he ao pāhorehore.
At night all are assembled; by day all are scattered.

The proverb is quoted by Īhaka, who wrote: 'At night, all are together for whatever is to be done (for example, clubs, meetings) but in the daytime, all scatter to their various work, or homes.' This is a favourite saying in the Wairarapa mainly applied to organisations. At first all are keen to form an organisation, but as time goes on, the faithful few are left to carry on the work.

Origin, doubtful
I motu mai i whea te rimu o te moana?
From what island does the seaweed come?

A saying applied to strangers.

Origins, mixed
Kotahi te taha mahimahi, kotahi te taha parāoa.
One side is of lowly birth, one side is of aristocratic descent.

Applied to a person of noble descent on one side of the family, and of lowly birth on the other.

Overwhelm, to
He kāpara miti hinu.
Rimu heartwood soaks up soil.

If you are visited by a chief and his followers, you will be honoured, but they will soon eat you out of house and home.

Pākehā
Kei muri i te awe kāpara he tangata kē, māna te ao, he mā.
Shadowed behind the tattooed face a stranger stands, he who owns the earth, and he is white.

An old prophecy made by a dying chief.

Parents
Matua pou whare rokohia ana, matua tangata e kore e rokohia.
A house-post parent (ancestral figure) may be found at any time, but a human parent may not be found so easily.

The proverb refers to the fact that death may rob one of one's parents at any time.

Parting
Haere! Matenga kē mōu, matenga kē mōku.
Go! Your death and mine will be in different places.

Said by Mania-uru-ahu to his daughter who chose a lover against her father's wishes. It was a way of saying that he did not wish to see her again.

Patience
E koa koe aianei, ā, māku hoki te rā āpōpō.
You rejoice today, but my turn will come tomorrow.

This saying was supposed to be used first by the tangata whenua, the original inhabitants of the land. After the Māori came, the first inhabitants were driven into the forest, and as they were seen so seldom, a belief grew that they were tūrehu, or fairies. When digging fernroot for food, the Māori would sometimes hear a voice saying the words that have been quoted, and, fearing what might happen, they took the first three roots they had dug and put them on one side as a gift to the tūrehu.

Āu mahi, e te kawau moe roa.
Your deeds, o long-sleeping shag.

Although a good illustration of quiet, persistent work which achieves results, the saying was applied directly to the set nets, eel pots and bird snares, which were called kawau moe roa, when a good haul was made. The shag remains very still, as though sleeping, until it sees the fish and, with a lightning dart, secures its prey. In a similar manner, the net remains quiet but secures the fish.

Payment
I paeārau koia au, kia hoatu kau taku mea mōu?
Have I been cast ashore simply that all my possessions should be given to you?

Implying that some return should be made to the speaker.

Me utu ki tō rae?
What is your face worth?

Do you expect to get anything from us? What have you to give in return? Only your face!

Te tangata i te whakautu whakanakonakotia; te tangata i te whakautu kore, ka tātahi.
The man who makes recompense is tattooed elaborately, the man who does not pay is done roughly.

Whakanakonako means to tattoo finely or closely; tātahi is wide apart. The man who pays little gets a cheap and inferior job.

Peace
Ko te paki nō Rūhī i horahia ki waho.
The fine weather of Rūhī is spread everywhere.

Peace prevails.

Maka e. E tae koe ki uta, kei mau ki tai ki Tū, pūhia he angina, e mau ki tai, ki Noho, e huhu, e pepe hanehane.
Hello, Maka, now do you mind, when you arrive on shore there, don't you have anything to do with fighting, or you'll be blown away like a cloud; but you hold fast to peace; let it be through worms and flies that your body falls to dust — do not let your enemies kill you and eat you.

The translation is by Grey. It is part of the famous farewell speech of Hou-mai-tawhiti as the canoes left Hawaiki on the great migration of the fourteenth century.

Winiwini ki uta, winiwini ki tai, taku waewae tipa ki te kura.
Terror on land, terror at sea. My feet are turned aside by red feathers.

Grey says that clothing of red feathers was a sign of bravery, and of peace won by personal courage.

Te aute tē whawhea.
The paper mulberry bark is not disturbed.

Introduced from Hawaiki, the aute provided a thin cloth which was so light that it could be blown away by the wind. When peace reigns, it is said that the aute bark is not disturbed.

A similar proverb reads:
Haere mai ki Hauraki, te aute tē awhea.
Come to Hauraki where the aute bark is not blown away.

Tatau pounamu.
The door of greenstone.

A figurative expression for an enduring peace, which was often cemented by the exchange of valuable greenstone heirlooms. An example of the use of the proverb is in a speech by the Ngāti Kahungunu chief Ngā Rangi-mata-ea:
Me tatau pounamu, kia kore ai e pakaru, ake, ake.
Let us conclude a permanent treaty of peace, that may never be broken, for ever, for ever.

He whakahou rongo wāhine he tatau pounamu.
Peace brought about by women is an enduring one.

Normally, in times of crisis, high-born women, puhi, were married to the victors to cement the peace and to ensure there would be no more warfare.

Peace and war
He pūkai tō Tū, he pūkai tō Rongo.
A heap of Tū, a heap of Rongo.

Tū is the god of war, whose heap is that of slain bodies. Rongo is the god of peace, whose heap is of kūmara.

He kōrero taua ki Wharaurangi, he kōrero tā matau ki Ōtuawhaki.
Matters of war are discussed at Wharaurangi, while at Ōtuawhaki they talk of making fish-hooks.

Wharaurangi was a flat rock opposite the Pōhaturoa rock at Whakatāne, where important decisions were made; whereas Ōtuawhaki was a place where fish were brought ashore. The proverb emphasises the importance of Wharaurangi.

Perfection
Ruia te taitea, kohia te kai rangatira.
Scatter the sapwood, gather up the chiefly food.

Ruia taitea, kia tū kō taikākā anake.
Strip off the sapwood, gather only the heartwood.

Perseverance
Ki te hāmama pōpoia te tangata, e kore e mau te ika.
If a man spends his nights yawning, he will not catch any fish.

The meaning is that work of any kind will never be completed if the worker gets tired of it.

Nā te waewae i kimi!
Look, the seeking feet!

It is only by searching diligently that one is able to make a living.

Ka tohe puruhi te tangata nei.
The man is as persistent as a flea.

He nui maunga e kore e taea te whakaneke, he nui ngaru moana mā te ihu o te waka e wāhi.
A great mountain cannot be moved, a giant wave can be broken by the canoe's prow.

Do not give up too easily — some things are possible.

Tohea, tohea, ko te tohe i te kai.
Keep on striving, as one strives for food.

Pin-pricking
He namu pea ahau.
Perhaps I'm a sandfly.

Though I'm small like a sandfly, I can be very vexing.

Plains
Anō nā te kāhu i hāro.
As if it were scraped clean by a hawk, or skimmed over by the wings of a hawk.

A saying applied to unforested country.

Pleasures
He ahi kouka ki te awatea, ā, he ai ki te pō.
Roasted fruit of the cabbage tree during the day, and the pleasure of a woman during the night.

Part of a famous conversation between Tapuwae and Taharākau. As J.H. Mitchell said, Tapuwae, not to be outdone by the modesty of Taharākau's reply to his question, said that his 'food' was:
He rā ki te awatea, he namu ki te pō.
The sun during the day, and mosquitoes at night.

Plotting
Ko Māui whare kino.
Māui of the evil house.

A figurative expression for a council house in which many plots and stratagems are laid. Māui was a deviser of many schemes.

Point of no return
E kore a muri e hokia.
There is no turning back.

Possession
Ka mau tā Māui ki tōna ringaringa e kore e taea te rūrū.
What Māui has got in his hand he cannot throw away.

When Māui fished up the North Island, his brothers begged him to let it go, but he replied in the words of the proverb.

Possession, communal
He waka eke noa.
It is a canoe which belongs to no one.

Nearly all property was held in common by the whānau, the hapū, and the iwi. If a man painstakingly made a canoe for his own use, his people could also claim it for their use by these words.

Possession, taking
Ko te papa, ko te papa.
It is victory, it is victory.

The English rendering of this brief rallying cry as given by Grey: 'Never mind your losses, never mind your losses; press on, press on, and get possession of the place.'

Possessions
He tangata momoe, he tangata māngere, e kore e whiwhi ki te taonga.
A sleepy man, a lazy man, will never acquire possessions.

Poverty
Ana ngā kai a Tama-tāhei, tērā kei tua o Kapenga.
All the food of Tama-tāhei has been sent beyond Kapenga.

The moral is that the giver has been so generous that he has nothing left to give away.

He mate kai e rokohanga, he mate anu e kore e rokohanga.
Suffering from lack of food may be supported, but to be cold cannot be borne.

Anyone who is hungry will be fed, but one who is cold because of lack of clothing will not get any help. The making of cloaks was a long and difficult task, and the needs of the sufferer were not so readily relieved.

Mau nā ko te wī, nā mau nā te pungapunga o Waikato.
You have nothing to offer but tussock-grass — nothing but the pumice stone of Waikato.

Ruatāhuna paka kore.
Ruatāhuna without the smallest particle.

A similar saying is:
Ruatāhuna kākahu mauku.
Ruatāhuna clad only in mauku cloaks.

Best says 'both of these sayings are used, not to express the sterility of the land, but the lack of any cultivatable food product . . . and the want of flax wherefrom to weave garments. The altitude was too great for the sweet potato to flourish, and no flax grew on those forest ranges, save a hill variety which contains a very poor fibre. Hence, sometimes, rough temporary mats or coverings for the body, were made from the fronds of the mauku fern.'

Ko te pokopoko o Rotu.
The ear-lobes of Rotu.

According to Grey this proverb means: 'We have nothing here in Rotorua to give you to eat, unless we cut off our ears for you.'

Power
Taranaki te tama a Mahirua, Te tāmure unahi nui, Te harakeke tō mai i roto o Waiwiri.
Taranaki the son of Mahirua — the big snapper scales, or the flax taken from the lake Waiwiri.

A proverb applied to a powerful tribe which is compared to Taranaki, descended from Mahirua, whose warriors were as numerous as the scales of the snapper, and plentiful as the flax of Waiwiri, which grew in such profusion that, when it was gathered, the multitude of bushes seemed as great as ever.

Kotahi nā Tūrāhiri ka horu te moana.
One of Tūrāhiri's men alone could cause the sea to roar.

Tūrāhiri was an ancestress of the Rongo-whakaata tribe, whose men were noted for their valour.

Precedence, order of
Tāria koe e ahu mai, kia mātaotao.
You will not come for a great while yet, until you are cold.

The saying refers to an important chief who will visit or give presents to others before he does so to the speaker. The proverb says that the basket of food will not arrive until it is cold.

Premature rejoicing

Whati mai, whati mai, Ka eke ki paepae poto a Hou, ki te puna whakatotō riri.
They came quickly, quickly. They arrived at the very threshold of Hou, and then the fountains of war gushed over.

A first advantage does not mean final victory.

Preparation

Kahore he tārainga tāhere i te ara.
You will not be able to fashion a bird spear on the road.

The bird spear must be made before leaving home, otherwise one will die of hunger.

E tata runga, e roa raro.
Above is close, below is long.

Kōhere translates it 'The sky is not far up, the way is long.' Best renders it: 'There is a long way to go, and the clouds are lowering. Let us make haste.' Īhaka explained that Taharākau, a high-ranking chief of Gisborne, and a companion, Te Angiangi, left Gisborne on their way to Te Reinga, near Wairoa. Te Angiangi, before their departure, clothed himself with all his beautiful garments, whilst Taharākau busied himself wrapping up his garments. Te Angiangi called out to his friend: 'Taha! Why are you taking so many clothes on such a fine day as this?' To this, Taharākau replied: 'Above is near, but below is far.' As they were approaching their destination, Taharākau began to chant an incantation, and before long, thunder was heard. Taharākau then began to unwrap his garments and clothed himself so thoroughly that there was no chance of his becoming wet. Presently heavy rain fell, and before long Te Angiangi was thoroughly wet, whereupon he called out to Taharākau: 'Taha, give me some of your garments; I am thoroughly wet and very cold.' In reply, Taharākau said: 'Did I not tell you that above is near, and below far away?' Immediately after this the rain ceased and the weather became fine. The moral of this proverb is that one should be fully prepared for all eventualities.

Presumptuousness

Kia mahara ki te hē o Maka.
Keep in mind the failing of Maka.

A warning against being too presumptuous.

Pretence

Whakaruapūtahanga i a koe.
You are making yourself out to be as great as your ancestress Ruaputahanga.

Ruaputahanga means a store from which supplies are constantly being drawn, and may be a figurative expression for generosity.

Prevention

Mokonahatia te waha o te kurī nei ki te mokonaha, kei haere, kei tāhae.
Muzzle the dog lest it should go and steal.

Preying

Me te waha kahawai.
Like the mouth of the kahawai.

Pride

Tōku toa, he toa rangatira.
My bravery is inherited from the chiefs who were my forebears.

Pride, false

He tupuna hoko pipi.
An ancestor paid for with shellfish.

At an important marriage ceremony, supplies of sea birds were provided in such quantities that the people became proud of their accomplishment. Other sections of the tribe made this contemptuous remark.

Pride, tribal

Ko Tongariro te maunga; Ko Taupō te moana; Ko Tūwharetoa te iwi; Ko Te Heuheu te tangata.
Tongariro is the mountain; Taupō is the lake; Tūwharetoa is the tribe; Te Heuheu is the man.

Probably the most famous of the many sayings in which a powerful chief is compared to a mountain. Cowan wrote: 'Tongariro, the sacred snow-clad volcano, and the great sea of Taupō were the only objects sufficiently grand and imposing to be compared to the god-like chieftain and high-priest Te Heuheu, who was killed in 1846, and whose son gave to the nation the Tongariro National Park.'

Kōhere has recorded a number of similar sayings:
Ko Hikurangi te maunga, ko Waiapu te wai, ko Ngāti Porou te iwi.
Hikurangi is the mountain, Waiapu the river, Ngāti Porou the tribe.
Ko Ruawāhia te maunga, ko Mokonuiārangi te tangata. Ko Pūtauaki te maunga, ko Rangitūkehu te tangata. Ko Whakapaukōrero te maunga, ko Rerehu te tangata. Ko Kahurānaki te maunga, ko Te Hāpuku te tangata. Ko Titi-o-kura te maunga, ko Te Rangihīroa te tangata. Ko Mauao (Maunganui) te maunga, ko Tūpaea te tangata.

Tūhoe moumou kai, moumou taonga, moumou tangata ki te pō.
Tūhoe, wasters of food, wasters of property, wasters of men in battle.

The Tūhoe tribe were proud and did everything on a grand scale — in the provision of food and hospitality and in war.

E kore e ngaro, he tākere waka nui.
We will never be lost, we are the hull of a great canoe.

Indicating pride in the might and numbers of a large tribe which can never be wiped out.

Privilege
He kai nā te ringaringa whero i taka.
Food prepared by the hand of a chief.

Red (whero) is a sacred colour, and therefore a figurative expression for a chief is whero, or ringa whero.

Procrastination
He tau ki tua.
Not now, some other time.

Hei te tau koroī rā anō.
Put off till the time when the berries of the white pine appear.

E tata mate, e roa taihoa.
Death is near, by-and-by is a long way off.

E kore te kai e whai i te tua o Hekemaru.
Food will not follow the back of Hekemaru.

If the inmates of a pā allowed him to go past before inviting him in to eat, Hekemaru would never turn back, because the invitation was then given to the back of his head, which was the most sacred part of his body.

Prodigal son
Kai hanu, kai hanu, hoki mai anō koe, koe tō kōiwi.
Oven food, oven food, you keep returning here.

Said of one who goes from place to place seeking food and entertainment, but always returns home when he has exhausted the patience of others. An idle, good-for-nothing fellow.

Progression
Ka tō he rā, ka rere he rā.
A sun sets, a day is born.

There is always someone to take the place of a dead leader.

Ko te pipi te tuatahi, ko te kaunuku te tuarua.
A small wedge is used first, followed by a larger one.

Small wedges termed pipi were used in splitting timber, and then larger ones, kaunuku, for bursting the wood apart. The proverb was quoted or explained by Elsdon Best in this form.

Promises, empty
Ngā kōrero o ērā rangi, mahue noa ake.
The words of other days are all left behind.

He waha huka.
A frothy mouth.

Applied to one who makes promises and fails to carry them out. Alan Armstrong points out that during the Second World War, Sir Apirana Ngata composed a song called '*Hitara Waha Huka*', 'Hitler the frothy mouthed.'

He pai kanohi, he maene kiri, he rā te kai mā tōna poho, Waihoki, he pai kupu kau.
A beautiful face, a pleasant skin, a breast kissed by the sun, such is an idle promise.

A woman, beautiful in appearance, who lies in the sun rather than work, is like a man who makes idle promises but will do nothing to fulfil them.

Hohoro i aku ngutu, e mau ana te tinana.
My lips move quickly, but my body is bound.

Promises are easily made, but not so readily fulfilled.

Poroaki tūtata, whakahoro ki tau kē.
You take your departure with words of farewell, but you will put off your return until next year.

Promises to return speedily are not fulfilled, a saying applied to those who make promises which they are unable to keep. Whakahoro, while meaning delay or put off, can also mean to slide or fall by degrees, like a slow-moving landslide.

Provision for the future.
Tukua atu ki tua, ki ngā rā o te waru e.
Leave it for the future, for the days when food is scarce.

'*Ngā rā o te waru,*' literally the days of the eighth month, is a colloquial expression for days of scarcity before the new crops are lifted. Grey says: 'Leave it for the by-and-by — for the long days of Summer; my revenge shall be so great that I must have long days to get it all in.'

Provisions
Ka haere Rangipō, ka haere Raeroa.
There goes Rangipō, there goes Raeroa.

The proverb sums up the tale of Rangipō and Raeroa, who went on a journey together. The former took the image of his atua with him, but the latter carried the god on his back and food in his hands, thus surviving while Rangipō perished.

Huakatoa anake i ora ai.
Huakatoa was the only one who survived.

Huakatoa took food with him on a journey, but his companions were not so prudent, and therefore Huakatoa was the only one who remained alive.

Provocation
He tohe tāu ki Kaiwere?
Are you persisting in trying to reach Kaiwere?

If I am provoked any further, the consequences will be serious.

Punctuality
E mua kai kai, e muri kai huare.
The first to come eat food, those who are left behind swallow spittle.

A rebuke by the chief Taimapuna to those who arrived late.

Pursuit
Te toka rurenga tai, neneke i te ngaru.
The boulder tossed about in the tide and shaken by the waves.

Applied to foes who are pursued relentlessly from one place to another.

Haere! Kia hiki ai koe i ngā kurī a Pohokura.
Go! Unleash the dogs of Pohokura.

A saying used of the warriors of Ngāti Huri of Maungapōhatu, who were famous fighters. Once they set out on the war path, no one could hope to escape them.

Quality
Ka whakarērea te pūhā, ka whai ki te matariki.
The inferior reeds are thrown away, the superior ones are sought after.

Toetoe or pampas grass was sometimes used in the construction of houses, the fronds for thatch and the stalks as linings for the house. There were two species: toetoe matariki, which was best suited for the purpose; and toetoe pūhā which, although larger, was crooked.

Quality, not quantity
He iti rā, he iti māpihi pounamu.
I may be small, but I am an ornament of greenstone.

The most prized of materials for ornaments was greenstone. Alan Armstrong comments that the Ngāti Porou chief Hikitai flung a spear during battle at Tamahae, the Bay of Plenty chief. Tamahae taunted Hikitai because he was short, and the latter replied with these words.

Quarrels
Nāna ki mua, nāku ki muri.
He began it; I followed it up.

Grey's version. Colenso quotes only the first three words which, he said, were always highly exculpatory.

Quarrelsomeness
He whiti ringa.
A ready hand.

Whiti means a shock, or a spring trap which closes suddenly on its victim. A hand that is always ready to strike a blow is the sign of a quarrelsome person.

He kurī kai tāwhao.
A dog eating scattered remnants of food.

Applied to a quarrelsome, interfering person. The warriors of Ngāti Huri were sometimes described in this way. *See* Pursuit.

Quickness
Me he muka tāpoto.
Like a superior kind of flax fibre.

The best flax could be cleaned quickly without scraping.

Quietness
Te papa nō Rotu.
The foundation of Rotu.

Rotu was emblematic of peace and quietness.

Rain

He ua ki te pō, he paewai ki te ao.
Rain at night, eels at dawn.

When it rains at night, eels may be caught the next morning. A figurative expression which implies that rain will disguise preparations for attacking the enemy.

Rainbow

Ki te kōmā te āniwaniwa, ka mate te tangata.
A rainbow, pale in colour, a man will die.

A light-coloured rainbow was an evil omen.

Tīwhanawhana ai Kahukura i te rangi.
Kahukura in a vast curve in the sky.

Kahukura was the god of the rainbow.

Ko Uenuku tāwhana i te rangi.
Uenuku like a bow in the sky.

Uenuku was also a rainbow god.

Rank

He aha te tohu o te taringa? He kawakawa.
What is worn in the ear? Kawakawa (a type of greenstone).

A question addressed to one who has seen a man pretending to be a rangatira. The questioner is throwing doubt on his claims.

Ransom

Me utu a Te Aka ki te aha?
What ransom must we pay for Te Aka?

As the young chieftainess Te Aka was restored to her people on payment of a piece of greenstone, how much less are you worth!

Recklessness

Mate wareware te uri o Kaitoa; takoto ana te paki ki tua.
The thoughtless sons of Kaitoa died; the fine weather followed immediately.

Kaitoa means reckless. The reckless young men put out to sea in a gale and were drowned; immediately afterwards the storm died down and the weather became fine.

A similar proverb reads:
Mate papa kore te uri o Kaitoa.
The children of Kaitoa died needlessly.

Recuperation
He pūreirei whakamatuatanga.
Pausing for a moment on a niggerhead.

Niggerheads are raised clumps of vegetation or reeds to be found in swamps. A traveller may rest on one for a while to get his breath before continuing on his journey. Colenso renders the proverb: 'A faithful, fatherly tuft of rushes'; but Grey's version of resting or pausing after an effort seems more likely.

Refreshment
Mā roto hoki kia ora ka pai te kōrero.
If the inner man is refreshed, the conversation will be agreeable.

Refuge
He pukepuke maunga, e pikitia e te tangata; He pukepuke moana e ekeina e te waka; he pukepuke tangata, e kore e pikitia e te tangata.
A man can climb a steep mountain; a canoe can climb mountainous seas; a man cannot overcome a great chief.

If a fugitive takes refuge in the hills, or flies to the ocean, he can be caught; but if he takes refuge with a great chief, he will be safe from pursuit. There is a play on the word pukepuke, mountain, in the original which cannot be brought out easily in translation.

Refusal
Nō hea hoki te whai aha, Kāhore he takutakunga o te whare, o aku ringa rānei. Nā wai hoki te whai aha? Kāhore i whai kauri, aha.
I have nothing at all to give, and I possess nothing. I have not even the simplest food in my house ready to hand. What have I to give? I don't even possess a piece of chewing gum — simply nothing!

Kauri is the term for kauri gum, which was chewed, or which, when burnt, provided a pigment used in tattooing.

Relatives
Tākina ōu kāwai, kia mōhiotia ai ōu tūpuna. E kimi ana i ngā kāwai i toro ki tawhiti.
He has come to claim us as relatives, has he? Well, the runners of a gourd plant must spread a great distance then.

Applied to a man visiting distant relations. The proverb apparently contains a play on the word kāwai, which means pedigree or lineage, and also a branch or shoot.

Reliability
He mahi nā Uetaha e hokia.
The work is Uetaha's, and it will be done.

Uetaha could be depended on to return and finish his work.

He karanga kai, tē karangatia a Paeko; he karanga taua, te karangatia a Paeko.
At a call to a feast, Paeko is not called; at a call to arms, Paeko is called.

Paeko is neglected in times of prosperity, but is appealed to in times of need. A number of fugitives had appealed to Paeko for help, but he remembered an earlier occasion when he had been slighted by the same people at the time of the division of food. He called to them from the shelter of his pā: 'When the call is war, the call is for Paeko; when the call is for food, Paeko is passed over.'

There is another version:
Karanga riri, karanga ki a Paeko, karanga kai, ka hapa Paeko.
Kōhere tells the story of what happened in the house of Tūkākī at Te Kaha in 1942, when a rush was made for the food set out in the marquee. Someone said that ex-servicemen could wait for the next sitting, and a voice was heard declaiming the proverb.

Religion
He amorangi ki mua, he hāpai ō ki muri.
A priest in front, the carriers in the rear.

When a war party went out the tohunga bore an emblem of the war god in front, while those who carried food and supplies were at the rear. It has been said that if one of the party were injured, contact with the amorangi would restore him to health.

Repetition
Ka rua hoki.
That's twice, as I have already told you.

Colenso states that it is used when a second statement by the same speaker contradicts the first.

Requests
Puritia tō ngārahu kauri.
Keep a firm hold on your pigment.

Grey expands the translation as follows: 'If it was charcoal from the kauri tree, it would be wise of you to refuse to give it, because you could put it in a piece of pumice stone, and bury it in the ground, and it would keep for years improving with age, and at last serve to tattoo your son with, but what I ask for, you cannot use now and it will soon spoil.'

Resignation
Ka mate taku waka.
My canoe is done for.

E taea hoki te aha te pā horo?
What can be done about a pā that has been defeated?

This can be compared to: 'There's no use crying over spilt milk.'

Responsibility
Nā wai te kī? Nāku, nāku anake.
Whose was the word? Mine, mine alone.

Said by the chief Kai-rangatira when wounded in battle.

Responsibility, sense of
E taru ana i tāku.
It will be done; it's my garden.

Taru is a patch of vegetation. Wī Mahunu, who was the originator of the saying, may have been reproached, and justified himself as a good worker by saying, 'Let it be; it's my garden.'

Restlessness
He tou tirairaka.
A fantail's tail.

Used of a restless person, especially those who are restless in meetings. The fantail uses its large tail to change direction quickly as it catches insects on the wing.

Reticence
Rauru kī tahi.
Rauru of one word.

Rauru was the son of Toi, and was notable as a wood carver and a man of few words. *See* Carving.

Return
Kātahi ka auraki mai ki te whānau a te mangumangu kikino, i te aitanga a Punga i a au e.
So now you return to me, who come from a black and ugly family; to me the child of Punga.

Said to a woman by a lover whom she has deserted, and to whom she has returned. Punga was the parent of lizards and of fish that were regarded as ugly and deformed, such as the shark and stingray.

Whati ngā ope a Mōkau.
Mōkau is the place at which war parties congregate.

The chief Hae, who accompanied a war party, was highly tapu. When the warriors were being entertained at Mōkau, he let his shadow fall across the food for the second time, thus making it unfit to be eaten. Another chief reprimanded him and ordered him to go home. This was the origin of the saying about Mōkau.

Reuniting
Ka āpiti hono, hei tātai hono.
Broken pieces are joined together and companies of men are reunited.

Revenge

Mā iro e kite.
The maggots will find him.

Revenge will be exacted on the enemy, whose flesh will be eaten by maggots.

Nā tētehi te tihi, nā tētehi te tokomauri.
When one man sneezes, another will hiccup.

If one man begins a quarrel, his enemy will be sure to retaliate.

Ā koutou whakanene waiho i te kāinga nei, tīkina te umu e tāpuke mai rā, hukea.
Let your private quarrels be left at home; go away and open the oven that has been covered over.

An appeal to forego revenge.

Ridicule

Kei runga Matawhāura, kei raro Korokitewao.
Matawhāura is above, Korokitewao is below.

Judge Smith puts it: 'Matawhāura is above, Korokitewao below, below (very much below)', and explains that Matawhāura is a high cliff which rises abruptly from Korokitewao, a sand bank on the shore of Rotoiti. When a gift is small, it is ridiculed by saying that the side of the basket containing the gift towers above the contents like Matawhāura towering above the beach.

He aha mā te kōpiri?
What has the cripple to say?

Smith puts it: 'What has this little go-by-the-ground to say?'

Kei pakaru te tahā raumati.
Beware of the shattering of the summer-grown calabash.

Probably a contemptuous reference to the thin skull of an enemy.

Risks, taking

Tēnā te ngaru whati, tēnā te ngaru puku.
There is a wave that breaks, there is a wave that swells.

Or: There's a sea that breaks, there's a sea that doesn't.

Rivers

Waikato horo pounamu.
The Waikato river, swallower of greenstone.

Referring not only to the green colour of the water, but also to the green-stone heirlooms captured by the warriors of the Waikato. The proverb was first used after the famous battle of Hingakākā, near Ōhaupō, when the Tainui warriors fought against those of Waikato and Maniapoto.

Waikato taniwha rau.
Waikato of a hundred monsters.

Symbolic of its great chiefs.

Rumours

Aweawe ana ngā kōrero i runga o Te Pīware.
From far out of reach come the rumours, over the mountain Te Pīware.

'Don't believe all you hear.' Colenso recorded his suspicion that Pīware had a figurative meaning, pī being young, downy nestlings, and any-thing viscous or sticky. The full meaning of Pīware could therefore be that reports floating in the air are light and downy, and are easily caught and held by soft, viscid surfaces.

Nā Tangokōrero pea koe i tono mai ki konei.
Perhaps it was Tangokōrero, the bearer of reports, who told you to come here.

A saying applied to a traveller who brings alarming news.

Satisfaction

Taku pai hoki.
That's what I wanted.

Scapegoat
Ko Nukutaumatangi, ko te hara, waiho te raru mō Rupe.
The offence was Nuku's, but it was Rupe who got into trouble.

Scarcity
Te rā o te waru.
The sun in the eighth month.

A proverbial expression used when provisions were scarce.

Scavengers
E hamu karaweta ana koe.
You are scavenging.

Scepticism
I haere mai pea koe i te kāinga, i a Te Arahori.
Perhaps you have come from the village of Te Arahori.

Said sceptically to a visitor who comes with unusual tidings. Colenso renders Te Arahori as Mr False-way.

He marama koia kia hoki rua ki Taitai.
A moon indeed, to return twice to Taitai.

Said to a man who promises to give a present the next time he comes.

Scrounging
He kai pawe.
A wandering eater.

One who wanders from place to place sponging off others.

Sea
Kāore ana he au ahi, kā pā he au moana e mate.
Smoke from a fire is soon gone, but a current from the sea causes death.

The word au is used in both phrases, but has the double meaning of smoke and current. The ocean currents cause death to canoes.

Sea attacking the land
Te ngaunga a Hine-moana.
The biting or gnawing of Hine-moana.

Hine-moana is the goddess of the sea. She is always biting into the land. The waves that roll on for ever against the body of mother earth are called the gnawing of Hine-moana.

Searching
Mā te kanohi miromiro.
If I had the eye of the miromiro!

The miromiro is a small bird which searches for insects in the bark of trees. The proverb is used to encourage anyone making a search for a missing object.

Ko te kairapu, ko ia te kite.
He who seeks will find.

The same proverb may also be found in the negative:
Ko ia kahore nei i rapu, tē kitea.
He who does not seek will not find.

Seasons, changing
Ka ahei rawa au ki a Rūaimoko, kotahi ngaruetanga ka whiti he tau kē.
I know the labours of Rūaimoko, who, simply by shaking the earth, causes the season to change.

Rūaimoko, a shortened form of Rūaimokoroa or Rūaumoko, the god of earthquakes, was the unborn son of Papa, the earth. His movements cause earthquakes, which were called Kumekume a Rūaumoko (the pulling of Rūaumoko), and were also responsible for the changing of the seasons.

Second string
Ka mate kāinga tahi; ka ora kāinga rua.
One plantation, death; two plantations, life.

A man with only one plot of ground to cultivate is in danger of starvation if there is a bad season; but with two plots, he is likely to have sufficient food to survive.

The same idea is applied in another way in the proverb:
Ka mate whare tahi; ka ora whare rua.

This proverb means that a man with only one wife to work for him may die of hunger, while a man with two wives grows fat. It may be noted that the word whare means the people who live in a house as well as the house itself.

Secrecy
Ka tukua tā Pirikohoi, ka purutia tā Marukouake.
When Pirikohoi opened up, Marukouake plugged up.

Pirikohoi was a man who let everyone know what he was doing, whereas Marukouake was secretive.

He nui pōhue toro rā raro.
The many roots of the convolvulus creep below the ground.

An allusion to the evil, hidden thoughts of the heart.

Security
He urunga e kore e whakaarahia hau kino.
A pillow that is not disturbed by a howling gale.

The saying was applied to the summit of Tongariro, which was so difficult to access that anyone taking refuge there was safe from his enemies. The mountain is compared to a sleeper who is not disturbed by the gale.

Haere ana koe, ko ngā pipi o te āria, Ka noho mātou ko ngā pipi o te whakatakere.
You are swept away like shellfish in deep water between two shoals. We remain undisturbed like shellfish at the bottom of the channel.

Āria is a place where the surf rages between two shoals, sweeping the pipi (cockles) into a deep hole.

Mehemea ko Hangaruru!
If only we were at Hangaruru!

The scrub and undergrowth were dense at Hangaruru, and provided safe hiding places from the enemy.

Self examination
Mātua whakapai i tōu marae, ka whakapai ai i te marae o te tangata.
First set in order your own courtyard before you clean up another's.

Hokia ki ngā maunga kia purea koe e ngā hau a Tāwhiri-mātea.
Return to the mountains to be cleansed by the winds of Tāwhiri-mātea.

One should know oneself and one's own tradition before presuming to tell people about theirs.

Self-reliance
He urunga tangata, he urunga pānekeneke.
A human pillow, a slippery pillow.

To depend on others may be fatal; it is best to rely on oneself. Armstrong believes that in this context urunga means the circumstance of joining or associating with, and that the proverb should be translated as 'An association with one's fellows must always be transitory; to join with the land is to have permanence.'

He kai nā tangata, he kai tītongitongi; He kai nā tōna ringa, tino kai, tino mākona noa.
You can only nibble at another's food; but with food that you have cultivated yourself, you can satisfy your appetite.

Colenso records the proverb as:
He kai tītongitongi kakī .
Food that is stinging to the throat.

Although this meaning is not given to tītongitongi in Williams, it is a graphic expression.

A well-known alternative version reads:
Ehara tā te tangata kai, he kai tītongi kau, engari mahi ai ia ki tewehnua tino kai, tino mākona.

Selfishness

E riri Kai-pō, ka haere Kai-ao.
Eat-in-the-night is angry when Eat-in-the-day comes.

The selfish man is angry when a generous one comes to share his food. Alternatively, a mean chief would deny food to a visitor, while the liberal man would go out of his way to serve him. Colenso said that Kai-pō was the common term for a mean, selfish person.

Ka mahi ngā uri o Tāne kōpae ahi.
Well done, descendants of Tāne who lie alongside the fire.

One who blocks the heat of the fire from others. Travellers lay sideways to the fire, and a camp fire was therefore called ahi kōpae.

Sensitiveness

Ngāti Pāoa taringa rahirahi.
Ngāti Pāoa of the thin ears.

As a criticism it implied that Ngāti Pāoa were sensitive to slights and insults. Rahirahi has the double meaning of thin ears, and attentiveness, or quick hearing.

Shame

Waiho mā te whakamā e patu.
Let them be subdued by shame.

The famous saying of Te Tahi-o-te-rangi.

Kōrero whakatū ana tētahi a Wāhiao; noho ana tētahi a Wāhiao me tōngā rā.
A certain person descended from Wāhiao stood up and spoke; a certain person descended from Wāhiao sat there in silence.

Grey says, 'Each of Wāhiao's two wives had children; each family went on a different war party; one family achieved a victory and returned victorious; the other family failed, and arriving home first had to sit in silence and shame, whilst their brothers stood up before the people to relate their deeds.' The proverb was used to excite emulation of such bravery.

Me rau whārangi te kanohi.
A face like a whārangi leaf.

The wharangi is a shrub, the underpart of the leaves of which is white.

Shamelessness
Rae tōtara.
A wooden person.

Tōtara is a hard timber. The saying is used of one who tells lies, or is shameless or brazen.

Shapeliness
Tōia ngā waewae o tō tamāhine, kia tau ai te tū i te ahi taipari.
Massage the legs of your daughter, that she may have a good appearance when standing before the fire on the beach.

Māori mothers massaged the limbs of their children to make them shapely. Kōhere says that when young women returned from diving for crayfish they stood naked before a fire on the beach to dry themselves before putting on their cloaks, and at such a time their limbs and bodies were shown to best advantage.

A similar proverb refers to the young women looking their best on the undulating country of Manutūkē:
Tōia ngā waewae o tō tamāhine, kia tau ai te haere i ngā pārae o Manutūkē.
Massage well your daughter's legs that she might come shapely to the plains of Manutūkē.

Shelter
Te whare o te matata.
The home of the fernbird.

The fernbird builds its nest in the shelter of thick bushes.

Ka maru koe i tōku pūreke, he kahu pītongatonga.
I will shelter you with my raincape, an impervious garment.

Te Wherowhero had made an appeal for refuge from his foes, and the chief Te Ota Peehi agreed and made this welcome reply.

Siblings

Mā te tuakana ka tōtika te taina, mā te taina ka tōtika te tuakana.
It is through the older sibling that the younger one learns the right way to do things and it is through the younger sibling that the older one learns to be tolerant.

Size

Mōkau ki runga, Tāmaki ki raro.
Mōkau above, Tāmaki below.

A saying to indicate the extent of the Tainui country compared with that of northern tribes. Naturally the expression originated among the Tainui people. The phrase was first coined to remind the people that the deaths of two chiefs needed to be avenged.

Skill

Ko te whai wawewawe a Māui.
The quick whai-play of Māui.

Originating in Māui's skill at the game of cat's cradle.

Slander

He pata ua ki runga, he ngutu tangata ki raro.
As a raindrop above, a human lip below.

Slander is likened to the constant dropping of rain.

He tao rākau e karohia, ka hemo; te tao kī werohia mai tū tonu.
A wooden spear may be parried, and the blow turned aside; there is another kind of spear which can be thrown, but which cannot be parried. The second spear is a metaphorical one of biting words.

An alternative form:
He tao rākau, e taea te karo; he tao kī, e kore e taea te karo.
A shaft of wood may be parried, but not the shaft of the tongue.

Slavery

He pai aha tō te tūtūa?
What good is it if one is a slave?

No matter how handsome or capable a man may be, what good does it do if he is a slave?

He wahine whakarongo hikihiki.
A female slave who hears the rites performed over her slain relatives.

'*Hikihiki i te au*' is part of the whāngaihau ceremony in which the hearts of the slain are offered to the gods.

Sleep
Ka tata te kai a Tūiti.
The food of Tūiti is close by.

Tūiti was fond of his bed. You, like him, will soon be asleep.

In a longer form:
Kei te kai pea i te kai a tōna tupuna a Tūiti.
Perhaps he is enjoying what his ancestor, sleepyheaded Tūiti, liked so much.

E moe tonu ana te tohetaka.
The continuing sleep of the dandelion.

A late sleeper is compared to the native dandelion which does not open its flowers until the day is well advanced. An alternative form is:
Kai te moe tonu te tohetaka.

He kōkō whakamoe, ka mate te tangata.
When sleeping like a tui, man will die.

The tui became sluggish on cold, frosty nights, and was easily caught.

Slipperiness
Kua kaheko te tuna i roto i aku ringaringa.
The eel has slipped through my hands.

Small things
Iti te kōpara kai tārere ana i te puhi o te kahika.
Small though the bellbird may be, it swings on the topmost twigs of the white pine.

He paku te ika i raoa ai a Tama-rereti.
It was a small fish that choked Tama-rereti.

Tama-rereti, the chief who was believed to have visited the Antarctic regions, was choked when eating a shrimp taken from the stomach of a fish.

E kore e mahana, he iti nō te pūweru.
There is no warmth, the garment is small.

A small war party is described in this way if it seems too small to be effective.

He panehe toki, ka tū te tangitangi kai.
A little stone adze will fell large trees.

Ultimately the cleared land will produce quantities of food.

Another rendering is therefore: A little adze well used brings heaps of food. Whakatangitangi is a large wedge used for splitting a tree.

Nā poto, nā pūhakehake.
Though short, you are filled to overflowing.

An excuse made by a big man for eating so much food.

Tini whetū e iti pōkēao.
A multitude of stars, a small dark cloud.

A small dark cloud can cover a multitude of stars. Similarly, a small body of resolute men can defeat a large army.

The proverb is quoted in another form:
He iti pou kapua ka ngaro, ka huna tini whetū i te rangi.
Though a cloud may be small, it is sufficient to obscure many stars in the sky.

Marangai-pāroa came to the assistance of the Ngāti Raukawa when they were hard pressed. The latter were appalled at the small number of their allies, whereupon Marangai spoke these words.

He iti hoki te mokoroa nāna i kakati te kahikatea.
The mokoroa grub is very small, but it eats the kahikatea tree.

Smoothness
Me he tapa harakeke.
Like the edge of a flax leaf.

Me he nīao waka.
Like the gunwale of a canoe.

The top edge of a canoe became polished by the movements of the hands and arms of the paddlers.

Me te kiri kiore.
Like the skin of a rat.

Usually applied to a woven garment.

Snow
Ka rukuruku a Te Rangi-tāwaea i ōna pūeru.
Te Rangi-tāwaea gathers up his garments.

Te Rangi-tāwaea was an ancestor of the Ngāti Porou tribe. The expression was used when Mount Hikurangi was covered with snow.

Solidarity
Nō te mea rā ia, he rākau tawhito, e mau ana te taitea i waho rā, e tū te kōhiwi.
In a very old tree you may be certain that the sapwood is on the outside, while the heartwood is in the middle.

Indicative of a well-organised tribe, with the older, reliable chiefs in the centre, and the younger warriors providing the external defences.

Ki ngā whakaeke haumi.
Ally yourself with those who have already banded together.

Haumi is the piece of timber by which a canoe is lengthened, or is the joint which strengthens it, and the word is also used figuratively for an ally.

Ehara taku toa i te toa takitahi engari he toa takitini.
My valour is not that of the individual, but that of the multitude. No one can survive alone.

He ora te whakapiri, he mate te whakatakariri.
There is strength in unity, defeat in anger.

Sons, quarrelsome
Ko ngā ngārara a Rauhina.
Like the lizards or monsters of Rauhina.

Rauhina's sons were as fierce and quarrelsome as monsters.

Speech, confused
Ko Taumata whakahēhē kōrero.
The confused utterance of Taumata.

Grey stated that Taumata was a 'contradictory person'. It might refer to someone who was wandering from the point.

Speed
E kore e mau i a koe, he wae kai pakiaka.
A foot accustomed to run over roots.

A man who is used to bush tracks will be speedier than one who runs only over flat, sandy beaches.

Tūwharetoa waewae rākau.
Tūwharetoa on stilts.

An expression used of this famous ancestor, who was noted for his speed when travelling.

Spring
Ka tangi te wharauroa, ko ngā karere a Mahuru.
When the shining cuckoo calls he is the messenger of spring.

The sound of the cuckoo's call announced the coming of spring. Mahuru was the personification of spring.

Stability
Me te kōteo mau kupenga.
Like the post to which the net is attached.

The proverb is applied to a chief whose influence welds the tribe into a cohesive unit, as a post or pole holds the net in position. Colenso also suggested that, as a net encloses fish, so a tribe that is supported by a powerful chief will enclose and capture its enemies.

Ehara a Hikurangi i te maunga haere.
Hikurangi is not a mountain that travels.

Te Kani-a-Takirau, the great East Coast chief, refused the Māori kingship with these words. The underlying thought is the legendary restlessness of the central mountains of the North Island. He also referred to his high descent by saying, *'Kua kīngi mai anō au i ōku tupuna'* — 'I am already a king by descent from my ancestors.'

Staring
Tirohia he moko.
Look at the tattooing.

Grey puts it: 'That's right, look at me — I have a tattoo on my face.' It is said to a person who stares rudely at another. As moko means both a pattern of tattooing and person, there may be a play on words in this saying.

Stars
Ngā kanohi o te rangi.
The eyes of the sky.

Ngā whetū heri kai mai.
The stars carry food hither.

The stars were believed to exercise control over growing crops.

He whetū nui a Pareārau, he wahine karihika, he wahine tīweka.
The great star Jupiter, an immoral woman, a wandering woman.

Jupiter is likened to a woman of loose morals who wanders at night.

Steadfastness

Te toka tū moana.
The rock standing in the ocean.

A military metaphor, used of a force which stands steadfast against attack.

Waiho i te toka tū moana.
Let it be a rock standing in the ocean.

Titiro tō mata ki a Rehua ki te mata kihai i kamo.
Look at the unwinking eye of the star Rehua.

The eye of the warrior must be steadfast and alert in hand-to-hand fighting.

E kore e riro, he tī tāmore nō Rarotonga.
The cabbage tree of Rarotonga is never carried away.

A chief of courage cannot be overcome. Tāmore has the meaning as bare or bald, as well as deeply rooted, and Best said: 'Able to withstand a gale like the branchless *Cordyline* of Rarotonga.'

Strangers

He kōtuku rerenga tahi.
A white heron whose flight is seen only once.

The saying is applied not only to a stranger but to one who is seen rarely. For instance, when Her Majesty Queen Elizabeth II visited New Zealand in 1953, she was described as a white heron seen once in a lifetime.

He toka hāpai mai nō ngā whenua.
A rock carried from another part of the country.

Applied to one who has come from a distance and is a stranger.

Kua ū mai tēnei tauhou, ki tēnei whenua tauhou.
This stranger has arrived at this strange land.

A saying applied to Marutūahu who was travelling in search of his father.

Streams

E kore a Parawhenua e haere ki te kore a Rakahore.
Parawhenua will not come out in the absence of Rakahore.

Parawhenua was the personification of water and mountain streams, while Rakahore was the personification of rocks; by which the Māori meant that mountain springs and streams would not flow if it were not for the solid rock from which they issued.

Strength

He iti, he iti kahikātoa.
Though little, it is still a mānuka tree.

Although the mānuka is not a tall forest tree, it is noted for the strength and toughness of its wood, of which weapons are made.

Ana tā te uaua parāoa.
There is the strength (or resolution) of the sperm whale.

A warning that the speaker is strong and will not tolerate opposition.

Ehara koe i te ringa huti punga.
It is no little thing, o arm, to haul up the anchor!

Tēnā ko te hopu a te ringa whero, e kore e tāngāngā, tēnā ko te hopu a te ringa iti, he aha te huanga?
The grasp of a chief cannot be loosened, but the grasp of an inferior, what is the use of it?

Ka mahi te hopu a te ringa whero.
How strong is the grasp of the chief!

Ringa whero, the red hand, is symbolic of a chief, and hopu is the token of his strength applied to some important task. The expression '*he ringa whero*' meaning 'a chief' comes from the fact that red was a sacred and chiefly colour, hence one would expect to find a chief's hand stained red after he had smeared red ochre on himself.

Strife

E horo rānei i a koe te tau o Rongo-mai-tā-kupe.
Can you cause the waves to be still on the reef of Rongo-mai-tā-kupe?

Can you put an end to strife?

Te mutunga a Tautahi, te koha a Rua.
The end of Tautahi, the endeavour of Rua.

Tautahi kept hold of the end of the stick, while Rua tried to wrest it from him.

Success

Ngā rākau tango mua a Manaia.
The weapons of Manaia overcome the first (of the enemy).

An expression applied to those who are successful in attaining their object first.

Succession

Ngā tamariki tāne ka whai ki te ure tū, ngā tamariki wāhine ka whai ki te ū kai pō.
Male children follow after the male, female children follow after the mother.

Sudden appearance

He toke koe?
Are you a worm?

As if you had burrowed under the ground and appeared without warning.

Summer

Ko Rehua whakaruhi tangata.
Rehua weakens man.

Kua tahu a Rehua.
Rehua has burnt, or kindled.

Rehua pona nui.
Rehua the big-jointed.

Rehua kai tangata.
Man-eating Rehua.

Rehua, who is really the star Antares, is regarded as a sign of summer, and his name therefore appears in all these sayings.

The second quotation is used on a hot day, and also appears in the form:
Kua tatū ngā waewae o Rehua kei raro.
The feet of Rehua have rested below.

The third may be interpreted to mean that in summer men become thin and their joints protrude. The last saying implies that the work of planting is over when summer comes and men are free to go off on raiding expeditions. The expression *'Kāore anō a Rehua i tatū ki raro'* ('Rehua has not yet alighted') is used when fruit has not formed on the trees.

Sunset
Ka tuhi te toto o Kaitangata.
The blood of Kaitangata is gleaming.

Rupe built a latrine in the heaven of Rehua. Kaitangata climbed up to it, caught hold of a loose beam and fell, his blood staining the sky. When the setting sun is red, this saying is quoted.

Superiority
E waru pū hoki.
E waru pū, tautahi.
Eight couples and an odd one.

As Grey puts it in free translation: 'O yes, I'm a fool and you're a fine fellow, I dare say; but I know that twice eight are sixteen as well as you do; or that sixteen and one are seventeen.'

Tā ngā hunga nunui hanga e.
They act like a company of chiefs.

Surprise
He kokoreke pūoho tata.
A counter-charge to bewilder the enemy.

Kokoreke pūoho tata is the term for a stratagem used in battle, which may be likened to the manner in which one is startled when a quail or kokoreke darts out of the undergrowth.

Surprise visit
He ihu kurī, he tangata haere.
A dog's nose, a travelling man comes.

Kōhere pointed out that travellers had no way of announcing their arrival in advance. To excuse themselves if they came at an inopportune time, they would say, 'As a dog's nose follows a scent, so a wayfarer looks for an open door.'

Sweetness
Me te wai korari.
Like honey of the flax.

Tale-bearing
Ka mahi te kākano whakauru.
Well done, man of two tribes!

Kākano whakauru means variegated in colour, and also a person who is descended from two tribes. Such a person carried gossip from one tribe to another.

Talkativeness
He kākā waha nui.
A parrot with a big mouth.

A talkative person is like a chattering parrot.

Akuanei ngā pākura a Hine-mākaho keho rawa atu ai i Takauhiroa.
Presently the swamp hens of Hine-mākaho will be screeching loudly at Takauhiroa.

Hine-mākaho was an ancestress of the East Coast tribes which have always been noted for their ability to talk.

Ka kō ngā kōpara a Rongomaitāpui.
The bellbirds of Rongomaitāpui are singing.

This chief had three daughters who were known for their talkativeness.

Me te tarakihi e papā ana i te waru.
Like cicadas chattering in the eighth month.

Vivacious conversation and chatter are compared to the voice of cicadas in the summer. The same proverb is applied to people when food is in good supply.

Tattooing
He tōngā kē tā te kōkā, he tōngā kē tā te kauri.
The mother fashions in one way, the kauri pigment in another.

Pigment derived from kauri is used in tattooing. The inference is that the natural appearance is improved by tattooing. The proverb is applied to education as well as to adornment.

Taunts
Whiti koreke, ka kitea koe. Haere whakaparirau i a koe, haere whakamanu.
You spring out like a quail, and I see you. Go and get wings for yourself, and transform yourself into a bird.

Titiro ki Ōpou, ki te pā o Kaitoa.
Look at Ōpou, the pā of Kaitoa.

Kaitoa was supposed to have lived at Ōpou near East Cape, but the saying is an amusing euphemism for a blunt 'Serves you right!' Kaitoa is a word expressing satisfaction or complacency at the misfortune of others.

Tears
He roimata ua, he roimata tangata.
Tears of rain, tears of men.

Both were shed over those who had died.

Temper, good and bad
Ka riro Taihā, ka kata Maero.
Taihā is angry, Maero laughs.

Both were chiefs of the Taupō district. Apparently the proverb was used by a person who was determined not to lose his temper under provocation, and as an admonition to another who was becoming angry.

Tenacity
Te kōura unuhanga roa a Tama.
The long drawing out of the crayfish of Tama.

Tama discovered that crayfish could be drawn out of their holes by pulling them steadily. Similarly, warriors are not easily dislodged, but by patience they are overcome.

Te pūtiki na Papawharanui.
The basket of the descendants of Papawharanui.

Papawharanui was the mother of Tūhourangi. The buried meaning is that as a pūtiki or basket is lashed tight, so the tribe was not noted for fertility of imagination, but for tenacity of purpose.

Testing
Me homai ngā hau o Rīrapa ki uta.
Let the exploits of Rīrapa be seen on land.

While in the fishing canoe, Rīrapa boasted of what he could do when ashore, and neglected the work in hand. The boaster is therefore being challenged.

Theft
Kiore kai kete.
Basket-eating rat.

A simile for thieves breaking in and stealing. Also applied to a war party breaking into a fortress.

Ka mahi ngā uri o Tama-te-kapua!
Well done, descendants of Tama-te-kapua!

Tama-te-kapua, who commanded the *Arawa* canoe on its voyage to New Zealand, was the 'patron saint' of thieves because of the occasion when he and his brother mounted on stilts and raided the poroporo tree of Uenuku at Hawaiki.

Alternatively the proverb reads:

Ngā uri o Tama whānako roa ki te aha, ki te aha.

The descendants of Tama-te-kapua have kept on stealing from one another.

Thinness

Ka rere ki Orutai.
So you are rushing off to Orutai.

Orutai was a place where food was scarce. The saying was addressed to anyone who was becoming noticeably thinner.

Thoughtlessness

Werohia i te poho o Huatare.
A challenge to Huatare's stomach.

Huatare, who had a prolific crop of fernroot, was visited by friends from the coast. They expected him to entertain them, but did not think to bring any of their sea foods with them. This was Huatare's way of reminding them of their thoughtlessness.

Thoughts

Ko Tāne pupuke.
Tāne is welling up.

Designs, thoughts and plans are springing up in profusion.

E huri rā o mahara, e Toi e.
O Toi, your thoughts are in a whirl.

Thrift

He tīraha kūmara na Uekāhia.
The kūmara basket of Uekāhia.

Tīraha is a large basket for holding kūmara. Uekāhia had a reputation for putting a few kūmara in his tīraha in such a way that it appeared to be full.

Thunder

Ka mahi ngā uri o Whatitiri!
Well done, descendants of Whatitiri!

Whatitiri was the goddess of thunder.

Rūaimoko, puritia, tāwhia, kia ū, kia itaita.
O Rūaimoko, hold fast.

According to some legends, Rūaimoko, the god of earthquakes and volcanic fires, was also in charge of thunder and lightning. These words from a war song were an appeal to the god to restrain the fury of the storm.

Time
He pākura ki te pō, he kākā ki te ngahere.
A swamp hen in the night, a parrot in the forest.

Both the parrot and the swamp hen mark the passing of time by their cries.

Titbits
He kai poutaka me kinikini atu, he kai poutaka me horehore atu, mā te tamaiti te iho.
Pinch off a little bit of the potted bird, peel off a little bit of the potted bird, but give the best part to the child of the family.

Kei pau ngā para toenga a te uri o Tama-ngū.
Do not eat the morsels left by the descendants of Tama-ngū.

It is said that Tama-ngū often hid some of the delicacies he could not eat during the meal, rising at night to have a secret feast. A person who put any titbits on one side said this to warn others against taking them.

Toetoe
He puanga kākaho ka rere i te waru.
The bloom of the toetoe flies in the eighth month.

Tools
He iti te toki e rite ana ki te tangata.
A little adze can do as much work as a man.

Travel
Haere i mua i te aroaro o Atutahi.
When you travel, go ahead of Atutahi.

Atutahi is the star Canopus. The advice to the traveller is to go on his journey before Canopus appears, while food is still plentiful.

Pipitori ngā kanohi, kōkōtaia ngā waewae, whenua i mamao tēnei rawa.
With the sharp eye of the white-breasted tit, and its quick feet, a distant land will soon be gained.

A saying to inspire the young, or to urge travellers on to their destination.

He ō kākā.
Light provisions.

There was a belief that the kākā or parrot picked up a pebble from the shore and carried it in his claw, nibbling at it from time to time. The traveller is recommended to take no more food with him than a kākā carries in its claw. This gave rise to the expression: '*He ō kākā*' for light provisions.

He ngenge kē anō te ngenge o te haerenga.
Tiredness from travel is a different matter.

Treachery
Uenuku-kōpako kai awe whare.
Uenuku-kōpako eats the soot from his house.

In other words, he killed his own people. Uenuku had killed his wife because she committed adultery.

E Tū, e Tū, tē rangona hoki te reka o te kai.
O Tū, o Tū, how can I possibly taste the sweetness of your food?

After a battle, the chief Tūhorouta asked Tāmaki-te-kapua to share some kūmara with him, but while it was being eaten, Tāmaki wounded the other who, before he died, uttered these pregnant words.

Treaty, broken
Ka taka te kōwhatu i Wahakino, ka tū te toka i Tākore.
The stone of Wahakino has rolled, the rock of Tākore remains immovable.

The saying is attributed to Tamahae, whose symbol was the rock Tākore at Te Kaha, while Wahakino, a rock at Whāngārā, represented another chief, Konohi. The two chiefs entered into a pact of peace which was broken by Konohi, who was thus reproached by Tamahae.

Tree felling
Kei te raweke koe i tō tupuna i a Tāne.
You are interfering with your ancestor Tāne.

Tāne was the god of the forest and was personified in every tree. Placatory rites had to be performed before trees were cut down.

Another saying was in vogue when the tree fell to the ground:
Kua hinga a Tāne.
Tāne has fallen.

Similarly:
Takoto kau ana te whānau o Tāne.
The descendants of Tāne are laid low.

Trepidation
Me he manu au e kakapa.
Like the fluttering of a bird.

Trifles
Kei mākū tōku kākahu. Ā mākū noa atu ka pā he wera i te ahi ka kino, tēnā he mākū i te wai horahia atu ki te rā, kua maroke.
Do not wet my cloak. Well, moisture will not harm it, but if it had been burnt in the fire, it would really have been damaged. If it is wet with water, spread it in the sun and it will soon be dry.

Triumph
Kei a au te mataika.
I have the first fish.

The first person to be killed in battle was called mataika. The words are the triumphant cry of the warrior who has the honour of having killed the first enemy.

Another common form of the expression is:
Kei a au te ika i te ati.

Trouble making
He ika haehae kupenga.
A fish tears the net.

Truculence
Kei te manu tute au kei te pae.
Like a bird jostling others on the perch.

Ugliness
Ko te whānau a Punga.
The family of Punga.

Punga was the god and father of reptiles.

Unconquerable might
Ngāti Awa, te toki tangatanga i te rā.
Ngāti Awa, the adze which loosens the sun.

Ngāti Awa is so powerful a tribe that it is like an adze which can dislodge even the sun.

Kāore e pau, he ika unahi nui.
A fish covered with large scales will never be eaten.

A proud boast of Taranaki. It may be that the Āti Awa and Ngāti Ruanui tribes are referred to as the large scales that protect the fish.

Unfaithfulness
I whea koe i te ngahorotanga o te rau o te kōtukutuku?
Where were you when the fuchsia shed its leaves?

When the tribe was attacked and many warriors fell, you were conspicuous by your absence. The kōtukutuku or fuchsia is a native deciduous tree. If a man who was absent when the tribe needed him most begins to boast, this proverb is quoted with bitter sarcasm.

Unity
He iwi kotahi tātou.
We are now one people.

A saying attributed to Governor Hobson when the Treaty of Waitangi was signed.

Unreliability
Ko Waitaha ngā tangata, ko kawe kē te ngākau.
The men are Waitaha, but their hearts are unstable.

The Waitaha tribe long ago was noted for its numbers and the bravery of its warriors. It is believed that this saying is applied to unreliable, vacillating men who are Waitaha only in name.

E rite koe ki te taunoka.
You are like the taunoka.

Taunoka is the native broom (*Carmichaelia australis*). This proverb is used of someone who is indecisive and unreliable.

He hoe kōnukenuke.
A crooked paddle.

Uprightness
Me he rākau māmore au nei, tū tonu.
Standing straight up like a tree without branches.

Me he tara-ā-whare.
Like the wall of a house.

Useful employment
Te wahie ka whāia mō takurua, te kai ka mahia mō tau.
Firewood is sought in winter, food is worked for all the year round.

The saying is an incitement to employ one's time and energies most effectively.

Uselessness
He kaha anō ka motumotu.
Like a broken lashing.

Used by a wife to her husband when her attractions cease to hold him. Grey expands it as follows: 'I'm like a rotten, broken rope — no longer of any use. My beauty and strength to labour for you are gone; you no longer value me. As a rotten cord can no longer fasten a canoe to a post, it is swept down the stream — so I can no longer retain your affections, and you love a younger wife.'

Vanity
Ko wai hoki koia te wahine pai rawa? Te wehenga atu anō i a muturangi.
Who now is the beautiful woman? All beauty was finished when she died.

A proverb used against a woman who was vain. Muturangi literally means the last of the chieftainesses. It was also used when anyone said that the old times were best, or that women were once more beautiful than at the present time.

Variation
E koekoe te tui, e ketekete te kākā, e kūkū te kererū.
The tui sings, the kākā chatters, the pigeon coos.

Vengeance
E mate ana i a au, e ora ana i a Te Waranga.
Though I die, Te Waranga lives.

An appeal from a chief asking another to avenge his death.

Haere! Waiho au mā te hau o te whakarua e kawe atu.
Farewell! Let the east wind bear me along.

A saying which promises vengeance.

Versatility
He ringa raupā.
A chapped hand.

A term for a man who does work of several different kinds.

Vigilance
Tama tū, tama ora, tama moe, tama mate.
He who stands, lives, he who sleeps, dies.

Originally this probably showed the contrast between workers and idlers. Colenso renders it pungently: 'Standing chief — living chief;

squatting chief — hungry chief.' Kōhere records an alternative form: *Mauri tū, mauri ora; mauri noho, mauri mate;* in which mauri is the life principle of a man. Nowadays most Māori use it to signify that one must work and be alert in a Pākehā world if one wishes to succeed.

Vindictiveness
Ngā uri o Kōpū-manawa-whiti.
The descendants of Kōpū-manawa-whiti.

Kōpū-manawa-whiti was noted for never overlooking an insult.

Virility
Ko Tūranga makau rau.
Tūranga of a hundred lovers.

The expression has been applied to several places, for example '*Tāmaki makau rau*', 'Tāmaki of a hundred lovers', meaning that it was a place which commanded men's affections because of its fertility and situation, and therefore became a frequented battleground. Tūranga is the original name for Gisborne, and Īhaka says that a more correct interpretation is: 'Gisborne, noted for its fertility', but that a correct rendering would be 'However old a man of Tūranga may be, he is fertile.'

Visitors
Te manu a Tāne.
The bird of Tāne.

An expression applied to one who arrives at dusk.

He tītī rere ao, ka kitea; he tītī rere pō, e kore e kitea.
A muttonbird which flies by day is seen; a muttonbird which flies at night is not seen.

Welcome visitors who come by day; those who arrive by night are enemies who come to attack and are not seen arriving.

Hohoro te kai mā tātou ākuanei tū ana raeroa, noho ana raepoto.
Let us hurry and finish up the food; when visitors arrive, the meal will be over.

The second phrase has been so translated by Best. Grey capitalised raepoto and raeroa, saying that Raeroa is a chief and Raepoto a plebeian, and translates the second portion of the proverb: 'Presently someone of more importance will be here and the Raepoto will have to sit and see them eat.'

Ka ngaro te kai, e mimiti tā tūwaewae.
The food is all gone, consumed by visitors.

E! E mano atu hoki ngā waru a Kaitahi?
Oh, do you belong to the many who return to Kaitahi in the eighth month?

An expression used of visitors who arrived in winter.

Ko te ure anake te mea haere i te pō.
Only the penis travels under the cover of darkness.

While Māori society is becoming more tolerant of people coming onto the marae after sunset, it is still considered unacceptable. It is under these circumstances that the proverb is quoted. It should be borne in mind that it is only during the hours of sunset to sunrise that the host people have time to themselves. During the hours of daylight they must be prepared to receive guests.

Voices, harsh
Kia āta whakawiri i te ngehingehi.
Do not twist the tourniquet.

A ngehingehi was a device made of plaited supplejack vine, and was used to crush hīnau berries. It emitted a creaking sound, and the saying was applied to someone who had a harsh voice. Smith said it was of a singer trying to squeeze out a high note, and rendered it: 'Gently there! Don't twist your ngehingehi too tightly!'

Me he pūtaratara.
Like a trumpet.

Ko te waha i nui, he iti te tangata.
Though the voice is loud, the man is small.

The pā at Maungakiekie (One Tree Hill) was attacked by a war party led by a small man named Tutunui. The taua was hidden in the mist, but the defenders could hear Tutunui's voice shouting orders to his men. When the fog lifted and Tutunui was seen to be a small man, he was mocked by the words quoted. It incensed Tutunui so greatly that he outstripped his men and was killed after a desperate fight.

Waiting in hope
Waiho i te rā raumati.
Waiting for the summer days.

Wakefulness
Tēnā ngā kanohi kua tikona e Matariki.
Here are the eyes affected by the Pleiades.

A saying applied to one who is wakeful at night.

Wandering
Ngā paenga rau o Waiwaia.
The many resting places of Waiwaia.

Waiwaia was an enchanted log which for many years drifted on the Waikato and Waipā rivers and out to sea. It was often seen temporarily stranded on shore and on the river banks and became a figure of speech.

Wanderlust
He takapau pōkai, ngā uri o Paheke.
The people of Paheke always have their sleeping mats ready for travelling.

Ko Manaia tūranga rau.
Manaia who appeared in many places.

Me te ihe.
Like the garfish.

The garfish jumps along the surface of the water, and epitomises the restlessness of a wanderer.

Ngā waewae haereere o Tokoahu, kei tua, kei ia whenua, kei ia whenua.
The restless feet of Tokoahu who travelled on and on from one place to another.

He rimu pae noa.
Seaweed drifting about.

A saying used by a wanderer to describe his restlessness. Colenso said that he had heard it used by a young lover who had been rejected, as he travelled from place to place to forget his grief. 'It struck me as being very poetical,' he wrote.

War parties
Ko Rotorua matangi rau.
The many breezes of Rotorua.

This refers to the many war parties which could be raised in the district.

Similarly:
Ko Tarawera hau rau.
The many winds of Tarawera.

Warfare
Ka tahuna te ururua ki te ahi, e kore e tūmau tonu ki te wāhi i tahuna atu ai; kāore, ka kā katoa te pārae.
When the bush is set on fire, the flames will not remain there in the dry brushwood; no, they will spread right over the plains.

Warfare cannot be confined to a few people. It will spread like a conflagration.

He wahine, he whenua, ka ngaro te tangata.
For women, for land, man dies.

These are the two principal causes of warfare. The succinct statement is a famous proverb.

An alternative form collected by Grey reads: *He wahine, he oneone i ngaro ai te tangata.*

Ka tuwhera te tāwaha o te riri, kāore e titro ki te ao mārama.
The gates of war are open, and man no longer takes notice of the world of light.

Once the battle lust is on a man, he is unconscious of anything but the fight in which he is engaged.

He kai kora nui te riri.
Warfare is something that spreads as quickly as a fire.

Mō te ata kurakura o Tū-mata-uenga, o Tū-ka-riri.
Fit for the red dawn of Tū-mata-uenga and Tū-ka-riri.

Dawn was the time when attacks were made on the enemy, and was therefore sacred to the gods of war.

He kō te aruhe ka taea e te tangata kotahi te amo, te whawhai nā te tokomaha.
Digging fernroot is the work of but a single man, but fighting is the work of many men.

Warmth
Ae, ngā rā o toru whitu.
Yes, the days from the third to the seventh month.

Tīkao of Rāpaki said that in springtime old people liked to feel the sun's rays on their skins, as it was then not too hot. They would lie against a takitaki or fence and repeat the old whakataukī which has been quoted. The period is from July to November.

Warning
Ka kite koe i tā te angaanga riri.
Pay heed to the retaliation of the chief who has been angered.

Grey translates the proverb: 'You had better not quarrel with me, your ariki . . ., or you will find out what evils my rage will draw on you.'

Kāti rā tō pēnei, kei tae kau tāua nei ki weriweri.
Stop acting this way, lest your hostility provoke us too far.

Colenso capitalises weriweri, and calls it Angry-dispute.

The name enters into another proverb:

Ka tae ki Weriweri, he tohe rarā tōna otinga.

When (two) arrive at (the place called) Angry-dispute, the end is actual strife.

Warning, final

Ko Tāmaki hokinga tahi.

Tāmaki returns only once.

Warriors

Kia mau ki tēnā! Kia mau ki te kawau mārō!

Hold firm! Be steadfast in the attack!

The last words of Maniapoto when his warriors performed a war dance before him. Kawau mārō is a movement in a war dance or an attack, and has been described as an advance in column. Maniapoto's words were an appeal to his people to conduct themselves fearlessly as warriors. *'Te kawau mārō'* eventually became the tribal motto of the Ngāti Maniapoto.

He tuki ūpokororo.

Beating the water to drive the grayling into the nets.

Warriors who are not fit to fight, but only to strike the water to drive the fish into the net.

Wastefulness

E haere ana koe ki Hurakia.

Perhaps you are going to Mount Hurakia.

A place where birds were so plentiful that no care was taken to prevent waste.

Mehemea kei Kaingaroa e kore koe e whiuwhiu i ngā kai.

If you were on the Kaingaroa plain you would not throw your food about so prodigally.

He uri nō te rango moumou kai.

A descendant of the fly which wastes food.

The proverb is used of anyone who is wasteful.

Watchfulness

E moe ana te mata hī tuna, ara ana te mata hī taua.
Though the eyes of the eel fisher might be closed in sleep, the eyes of the sentry are always awake.

While the eel fisher is asleep, the warrior on the watch tower is alert. Colenso puts it graphically: 'The eyes and thoughts of the fisherman enjoy peaceful rest at nights, and he even nods between his bites when fishing; but those of the planner and conductor of battles know no rest.'

Ka mahi te kanohi kai mātārae.
Well done, the eye that watches the headland.

Applied to a person who watches steadily for any purpose, as those who watch the pools among the rocks below the headland, until the tide fills them and fish are trapped.

Mātai rore au ki te taumata.
Examine the snares on the hilltop.

Water

He huahua te kai? E, he wai te kai.
Are preserved birds the best food? Ah no! Water is.

Waves

Kātahi anō ka tūkari te māra a te Noinoi.
Now for the first time the plantation of Noinoi is being dug over and thrown into heaps.

A saying used when the sea begins to rise.

Weakness

He kōura kia wē te whero.
The water makes the crayfish red.

The meaning is that boiling water soon turns the crayfish red. The saying is applied to a person who is quickly overpowered by superior force. The same expression is used by an impatient man who soon comes to blows with his opponent.

Ehara i te uaua tangata, otirā he uaua kiore.
He doesn't have the strength of a man, but only the strength of a rat.

He whakarapa tō koutou, he tikanga hauhauaitu tō koutou nei.
You are unlucky, you are always too weak to carry anything to a conclusion.

Wealth
He peka kai, he peka taonga.
Some food and property, these are what a man needs.

He tukemata anō tō te taonga.
A fierce look succeeds in winning wealth.

Kōhere renders the proverb: 'Even wealth at times frowns.' Grey says: 'As a warrior's terrible eyes gain their victory for him, so the influence derived from wealth gains men what they desire in the world.' The true meaning, however, seems to be that fierceness or confidence impresses, and is the equivalent of 'Fortune favours the brave.'

Weather
Ka tangi te kārewarewa ki waenga o te rangi pai, ka ua āpōpō; ka tangi ki waenga o te rangi ua, ka paki āpōpō.
If the bush-hawk cries on a fine day, it will rain on the next day; if it cries on a rainy day, it will be fine on the next day.

He rā kōpanipani.
A cloud-enshrouded day.

He ua nehu ka patua.
If light rain falls as a war party sets out, it is an omen that it will be defeated.

Ko te rā māeneene a te rāhui Tangaroa.
This is a calm day for the flocks of Tangaroa.

Tangaroa was the god of fish. The proverb indicates that the day is calm and sunny.

Te paki o Rūhia.
The fine weather of Rūhia.

Rūhia was the child of Rehua, who betokens the warmth of summer. There are many such expressions for fine weather, for example *te paki o Hewa; te paki o Rangi; te paki o Autahi. See* Anxiety and Summer.

Me te rangi i whānau ai a Te Rangi-tauarire.
Like the day that Te Rangi-tauarire was born.

An expression for a fine day. Te Rangi-tauarire was noted for his pleasant disposition.

A similar saying for an unpleasant day was:
Me te rangi i whānau ai a Horu; for Horu was of an unpleasant disposition.

Again:
Mehemea ko te rangi i whānau ai a Te Tuarāriri.
Like the day when Te Tuarāriri was born.

Both proverbial expressions were used of a baby born on a stormy day.

Best records a modern variant:
Me te rangi i whānau ai a Hātana.
Like the day on which Satan was born.

Weaving
Ka mahi koe te whare o te mata.
You are making a nest for the fernbird.

This was said to a woman engaged in weaving a cloak of undressed flax leaves. The mata or fernbird builds its nest amongst the flax bushes of the swamps. There are several sayings of the same kind. One who is making a cloak of kiekie leaves is making a nest for the tieke or saddleback, which builds its nest in a bunch of these leaves. One who is weaving a cloak of toetoe leaves is building a nest for the pītongatonga, a small bird which frequents the toetoe. Toetoe leaves are strong, and the word 'pītongatonga' also means thick or impervious. Such garments make good rain capes.

Weeping

Ko roimata, ko hūpē ngā kaiutu i ngā patu a tēnei tangata nui, a Aituā.
Tears and discharge from the nose are the avengers of the blows of this great personal calamity.

Aituā are the personifications or causes of sickness, trouble, misfortune, accidents and evil omens. The quotation is used in speeches of mourning.

Welcome

Haere mai rā, e te manuhiri tūārangi.
Welcome to the guest from afar.

Whiteness

Me he pipi taiari.
Like the shell of the pipi.

Pipi taiari were used for necklaces.

An alternative version:
Me te kokota.
Like a mussel.

Wiles

Tangaroa ara rau.
Tangaroa of the many paths.

Grey states that the saying is used of enemies whose line of route is not known, or to anyone with many wiles. The proverb is based on the habits of eels which move by so many paths that, although the creeks at the head of a river are filled with eel pots, plenty of eels will still be caught further down the river.

Winter

Ko makeremumu hūpē tautau.
In winter when a discharge hangs from the nose.

Ko takurua hūpē nui.
In winter large drops hang from the nose.

These expressions indicate intense cold.

Matariki tāpuapua.
Winter, when pools lie everywhere.

Matariki or the Pleiades first appear in the month of June.

Te pō tūtanga nui o Pipiri.
The division of the long night of Pipiri.

At the time when the star Pipiri is seen there is a long division between evening and morning.

Wisdom
Haere e whai i te waewae o Uenuku, kia ora ai te tangata.
Good fortune comes to a man from the memory of going to the feet of Uenuku.

Uenuku was famed for his wisdom, which he passed on to others. A man who had sat at his feet gained knowledge which preserved him in all difficulties and dangers.

Wishful thinking
He manako te kōura i kore ai.
Wishing for the crayfish won't bring it.

The saying arose through an amusing incident. The chief Hikairo took refuge in his pā, and one of the raiding party exclaimed, 'There goes a fat meal for us!' The proverb was the reply made by Hikairo.

Wit
Ngā kōkō tātaki o Te Akatea.
The witty speakers of Te Akatea.

Kōkō is a name for the tui, and Best said that in the Waiapu district the male bird is called tātaki. According to him, therefore, talkative persons are compared to the noisy tuis of the place named Te Akatea. The usual explanation, however, is that a kōkō tātaki is a proverbial expression for a witty speaker.

Ko te tangata hua ana whakataukī, ko Tūraungatao.
Tūraungatao was a man well known for his witty sayings.

Wives

Kei mau ki te pou pai, he pou eketia e te kiore. Tēnā ko te pou kino, e kore eketia e te kiore.

My son, when you are building a storehouse for your provisions, do not put it on a fine new post; rats seeing such a post will think there is something on top of it, and will try to climb it; you, knowing this, will be always anxious about your provisions; but if you take an old, indifferent post, you will know that the rats will not be tempted to climb it, and your heart will be at rest.

Grey has provided the extended explanation of this short, cryptic proverb, the real meaning of which is that a young man will be much happier and free from jealousy if he chooses an older woman without pretensions to good looks instead of a younger and more beautiful woman as his wife.

Kia kino te tahā, kia tū noa ai i te marae.
An unornamented calabash may safely be left outside.

Similarly, a plain-looking wife is safe from the attentions of other men.

Aitia te wahine i roto i te pā harakeke.
Marry the woman in the flax bush.

If a woman is frequently seen gathering flax, it is an indication that she is a weaver. As such she is eminently eligible and should be preferred as a spouse.

Women

He kahawai ki te wai, he wahine ki uta.
A kahawai (fish) in the water, a woman on land.

Two meanings can be given to the proverb — the capriciousness of women, or the unpredictability of men in choosing their wives. The kahawai was noted for taking only the bait which resembled its normal food. Similarly, a woman is difficult to please, especially when it comes to choosing a man.

Haere atu te wahine, haere maro kore.
The woman goes, and goes without her kilt.

If a woman marries a man of another tribe (*he tangata kē*) she forfeits all rights to land in her mother's tribe.

Women, attractions of
He pai tāne e kore e reia, he kino wahine ka reia.
A handsome man will not be sought after, but a plain woman will be run after eagerly.

Nā tō tamāhine pai i tākina mai ai tēnei kekeno ki konei.
It was this lovely girl who brought the seal here.

Visits were often made by sea, so the beautiful young woman draws lovers to her as though they were seals coming in from the sea.

Women, deserted
He kaka tīhorea he tohu nō te wahine mahue.
A discarded garment is the sign of a deserted woman.

A deserted woman is like a discarded garment.

Women, the responsibilities of
He puta taua ki te tāne, he whānau tamariki ki te wahine.
The battlefield for man, childbirth for woman.

Words, hurtful
He kupu matangerengere.
A disagreeable word.

Colenso says that the expression has the meaning: 'A word having a hideously ulcerated face.' But this is only the literal interpretation of the component parts of matangerengere, which as a whole means harsh or disagreeable.

Words, not deeds
Ka roa te ngaromanga, he iti te putanga.
When it is hidden for a long time, it will be small when it comes forth.

The proverb is used of a man who has a great deal to say but who does not put it into action. It is also used of war parties which, when they are small, hesitate to come out to show their strength.

Work
Ihu oneone.
Good worker.

Although not strictly a proverb, it is a term with the wit and tang of a proverb. Ihu means nose and oneone means soil. Literally the expression is dirty nose, and indicates a person who is working hard and bears the marks of toil. A comparable English expression would be: 'Nose to the grindstone.'

Kia noho i taku kōtore, kia ngenge te pakihiwi.
Sometimes sitting on your buttocks, sometimes exhausted by the work of your shoulders.

Applied to paddlers in a canoe.

Pai tū, pai hinga, nā wai, nā oti.
Good at standing, good at falling, the work is eventually finished.

The thought is that whether it be well done, or badly, eventually it comes to an end.

Takoto kau ana te whānau a Tāne.
The children of Tāne lie prone.

A saying indicating that once the trees are cleared away, the work is done. It is applied to any work that is completed. In mythology, forest trees are the children of Tāne.

Anō me he whare pūngawerewere.
As if it were a spider's web.

A saying applied to fine and intricate work in carving or weaving.

He rā whatiwhati kō.
A day for breaking the spade.

An expression used for a day when everything is right for hard work. The kō was a long-handled digging implement.

Tēnā te ringa tango parahia.
This is the hand which pulls out the weeds.

Applied to a hard worker. In some places the kūmara plantations were overrun by a small plant called parahia, which had to be kept weeded in order to give the kūmara plants room to grow.

Workers
Ka mahi te hukuroa i ana mahi.
Well done! The band of toilers keeps on working.

Workmanship, bad
Ngā uri o Rongomai toki kino.
The descendants of Rongomai, who handle the adze badly.

Yearning for a loved one
He manu aute e taea te whakahoro.
A kite which, when slackened off, flies away.

A lover compares himself to a kite and longs to be released in order that he may fly to his loved one.

An extended version reads:
He manu aute au e taea te whakahoro ki te aho tāmiro.

Youngest son
He pōtiki whakahirahira.
The last-born, with a good opinion of himself.

The youngest son was often spoilt, ambitious and self-opinionated.

Youth
Ka pū te rūhā, ka hao te rangatahi.
The old rags lie in a heap, while the net is used for fishing.

When the old net is worn out and cast aside, the new net is put into use. The saying was applied to the Young Māori Party in its heyday.

Ka haere te tōtara haemata, ka takoto te pukatea wai nui.
The tōtara chips float while the pukatea lies in deep water.

YOUTH

Young people may travel, while older people are forced to stay at home.

Mahia ngā mahi kei tamariki ana.
Make the most of your time while you are young.

Index